FROM BENGAL
TO THE CAPE

FROM BENGAL TO THE CAPE

Bengali Slaves in South Africa from 17th to 19th Century

ANSU DATTA

Xlibris Corporation
1-800-618-969
www.Xlibris.com.au
Orders@Xlibris.com.au
502429

CONTENTS

Tables	Page

PREFACE

Ansu Datta, sociologist and Africanist of a high order, had begun this research on Bengali slaves, especially women, bought and brought to South Africa, some years ago in Cape Town. Come to know of it from him, whom I had met after decades in connection with a volume I edited to which he contributed, I realized its importance in slave as well as population studies and suggested that he wrote a book on it. To compare notes, I referred him to a current Bengali novel built around the female slave traffic of about the time of his interest on the Bengal and Orissa coast. At my instance he had a talk too with the author regarding the latter's sources. A long African sojourn and familiarity with the South African human geography were also conducive to him. The first draft was ready before long. There was an opportunity to try it out with a social sciences research group in Kolkata, and the response was most encouraging giving him every reason to put the final touches to his work and publish it. I even requested him to write a Bengali version of it so that the story could be available to the common Bengali reader. He assured me that he would do that after revising his English version. The revision did take a little time, for besides his text he had to spruce up the appendices. He might have done more, as was his wont, but his body didn't allow him. He fell ill with his manuscript on desk and passed away without seeing it in print. Our mourning for this gentle and perfect scholar, a rare human being, knew no bounds.

We are grateful to Xlibris for publishing it online and, thus, for its generosity in letting us remember him. I am writing these words as a former colleague at Jadavpur University, Kolkata where Ansu Datta had begun his teaching career.

Amiya Dev
Retired Professor of Comparative Literature
Jadavpur University, Kolkata

PS.

The above preface needs a small addition. It is likely that discrepancies, omissions or mistakes have occurred in the process of things being put together by someone who is not the author. For that I, his wife, take full responsibility.

Secondly, a couple of documents listed in the contents of the manuscript had to be left out since their sources were not located in the author's many papers.

Finally, the contents of the book have been slightly rearranged. The author had felt that the documents listed were too important to be appended separately. But since these documents were not yet woven into the main text by the author, the only way to include them is as appendices. The readers may like to keep this in mind.

Large number of women and men were taken as slaves from Bengal to the Cape of Good Hope by the Dutch East Indies Company from the seventeenth to the nineteenth century. Yet very few of their descendants are aware of their Bengali roots. Professor Datta has left behind extensive notes on sources he had unearthed, along with information on other archives, which could be explored and exploited. It was his opinion that further useful work might be undertaken in this area. This book would have served its purpose if future scholars pick up the trail of the new direction charted by this author into a new aspect of slave trade and slavery in South Africa that deserves research and acknowledgement

The map of the seventeenth century transoceanic trade routes of the Dutch East Indies Company, VOC, has been included in this book with the kind permission of Dr. Jean-Paul Rodrigue, Hofstra University, New York. For this I am really grateful to him.

Kusum Datta
Email: *kusum727@hotmail.com*
Kolkata, India

Maps

1. The Cape of Good Hope in the 18th century
   javascript: Zoom('3032B12_to_323_plaat_Hottentots.jpg',%20'en')

http://www.atlasofmutualheritage.nl/detail.aspx?page=dafb&lang=en&id=6413

2. Transoceanic VOC slave Trade Routes in the 17th Century

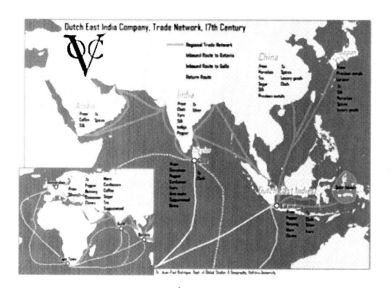

Source: http://people.hofstra.edu/geotrans/eng/ch2en/conc2en/map_VOC_Tr

CHAPTER 1

Introduction

There have been several studies of African immigrants coming to India across the Arabian Sea. Some such immigrants were recruited and employed as soldiers by Hindu and Muslim rulers, as well as by Portuguese, French, and British colonial administrations. A few are known to have come as free merchants. Others were slaves brought to India under duress.

African immigrants were, and still are, known, generally, as 'Habshi'. The word, derived from Abyssinia, modern-day Ethiopia, referred to the people from East Africa, especially from the Horn of Africa. Another common name for these people is *Siddi* or *Sidi*, the origin of which is debated. According to Suniti Kumar Chatterji (reprint 2004: 66) and Richard Pankhurst (2000), the term is a corruption of the Arabic word *Saidi* ('my lord' in English). How this word was later used in India to connote 'former slaves' remains a socio-linguistic puzzle.

Pockets of Siddi settlements have been found in western India: Gujarat, Karnataka, and the Hyderabad region of Andhra Pradesh. According to one estimate, the Siddis in India currently number about 30,000 (Van Kessel, 2006: 461).[1] Interestingly, 'Siddi' (alternatively, Zanzibari) communities have also been found in Kwazulu-Natal, more precisely, Durban (Kaarsholm, 2008: 9-10).

In Indian historical records, we find various references to African slaves. In the first half of the thirteenth century, Queen Razia's clandestine romance with an African slave led to tragic results. In the East, the offspring of African slaves ruled Bengal for a short period. Habshi rule in Bengal is generally traced to the reign of Ruknuddin Shah in the second half of the fifteenth century. Habshi power reached its peak during the last two decades of the fifteenth century when there were four successive Habshi sultans in Bengal. (Subramanyam, 1990: 118-19). Later, on the west coast of India, Habshi power emerged as a force to be reckoned with when the Siddis established themselves at a fort situated at a coastal village in Raigad, Maharashtra, locally known as Murud-Janjira. This is said to be the only fort along India's western coast that remained 'free' in the face of Maratha, Dutch and English East India Company. In actual fact, however, Siddis acted as feudatories of various political authorities on the Indian mainland, including the Mughals, but are said to have made a living mainly through piracy and coastal shipping.

Few Indians are aware of the forced migration in the opposite direction, i.e. export of Indian slaves to Africa. We find a mention of slave women from India exported to Sokotra Island in the Arabian Sea in *Periplus of the Erythrean Sea* (cited in Chanana's Bengali translation 1995, pp. 143-44). There may have been other such cases. Unfortunately, there is little information about forced migration of Bengali (and other Indian) slaves to Africa, more precisely to the Cape Province in South Africa. It is known now that this process started in the seventeenth century and continued for more than two hundred years. Slaves were procured principally from three regions: Bengal, the Coromandel Coast, and Malabar.

The present study focuses on the slaves of Bengali origin and deals solely with what is usually described as chattel slavery. Chattel slaves were acquired in their native lands and were forcibly taken to different places where they could be sold and made to work for others. This is the form of slavery that was prevalent in the Cape Colony and the Americas and is to be distinguished form indentured labour.

The spirit of the present study may be best prefaced with an observation made many years before by Haraprasad Shastri, a nineteenth-century social historian of Bengal: 'The Bengalis are a self-forgetting people' (2000: 268, 274 and 280). Before going to South Africa, the present author was completely unaware of the forced movement of hundreds of slaves from Bengal and nearby regions to the Cape. A recent visit to South Africa drove home the point made by Shastri with singular veracity. A chance engagement in the National Archives of Cape Town revealed to him in no uncertain terms that, in the seventeenth and eighteenth centuries, the economy of the Cape Province depended to a considerable extent on Bengali slaves.

Unlike slaves descended from some other ethnic groups, Bengali slaves have now been fully assimilated into the mainstream of Cape society. Following Orlando Patterson (1979: 39), we may call this process a kind of 'social death' or 'secular excommunication', in the course of which some slaves have become part of the white population, while probably a majority have been absorbed into Coloured communities depending on the physical features and cultural acclimatisation of the progeny of the original Bengali slaves. I guess an indeterminate number of the offspring of Bengali slaves is part of the black population, but there is no way to avow it with any certainty. Understandably, the process of absorption coincided with the generation of a new kind of identity through social rebirth, however incomplete. But, currently, descendants of Bengali slave population have little distinctiveness to make them singular in the 'rainbow nation'.

It should be mentioned here that acceptance of the slave status was facilitated by the recognition by Bengali slaves that the institution of slavery had an acknowledged position in their society of birth. *Manusamhita,* the ancient book of Hindu laws (third century B.C.E.), spoke of seven types of slavery: prisoners of war, those who are enslaved for their sustenance, those born in their master's house, those who are purchased, those inherited as part of patrimony, those who are given away by their parents, and those who fail to repay a fine or in execution of a judicial decree. As far as Bengal is concerned, slavery was an accepted institution so much so that the ancient treatise that governs the inheritance system of Bengali Hindus (*Dayabhaga*) recommends how a slave should be inherited. This was largely true of other ethnic groups as well.

In South Africa, slave contribution to the making of the nation was not fully recognised until recently, and people tended to forget that slaves played an important role in the country's history. Slaves outnumbered burghers in the Cape Colony for most of the eighteenth century. The economy of the Colony depended largely on slave labour. On top of it, many South Africans, of all races, descended from slaves, although this is often conveniently forgotten.

Currently, some serious attempts are being made to locate and re-interpret the history of Cape slavery (Sarah and Coetzee, 2nd impression 1999; *Towards A New Age of Partnership* or TANAP[2]). As part of this initiative, there are references to Bengali slaves (along with slaves of other ethnic groups) in documents, history books, and fictional writings. But there is little awareness in India and even among people of Indian origin in South Africa of the existence in Cape society of a sizable number of Bengali slaves two hundred years before.

[handwritten: Every historian's claim. Nonsense.]

Partly this [amnesia] is due to the 'Afrocentric' focus of the historiography of slave trade, in which Indian Ocean operations have suffered from a 'history of silence' (Vink, 2008: 2). This is reflected in the absence of an exhaustive history of the organisation of Dutch slave trade in Bengal. In retrospect, this bias of the historiography is not difficult to explain. In the first place, the archival work needed for this research was and still is a very difficult task because the sources are so diverse linguistically, which are spread over in the national archives of the major players (Dutch, British, French, and Portuguese) *[handwritten margin: Archival record]* at The Hague, London, Paris, and Lisbon. Supplementary materials are available in the assorted archives in Indonesia, India, and South Africa because the numerous settlements of the *Verenigde Oost-Indische Compagnie* (VOC) (1602-1799) kept records separately. Secondly, researchers preoccupied with Asian colonial history have focused on indentured workers. After all, export of indentured labourers from Asia happened later, and records of such population movements are richer and more easily available. Finally, studies of the Dutch East India Company period (1602-1799) tended to neglect slave trade because slaves accounted for a very small portion of the total value of Company's trade (0.5%) at the height of Dutch-dominated transoceanic trade (Vink, 2008.).

Ideally, an account of slave trade in this region should include detailed and systematic information on how slaves were acquired, whether they were taken directly to the Cape, or transported via Batavia (modern Jakarta), the Asian headquarters of the United Dutch East India Company (*VOC*), or any other trading outpost, and, finally, once brought to the Cape, how they were disposed of.

[handwritten: Fair enough point, but not very original.]

CHAPTER 2

Export of Bengali Slaves to the Cape

There have been some studies of the exploits of the Dutch East India Company in India (Das Gupta, 1979; Prakash, 1984, 1985; Ray, 1998; Raychaudhuri, 1962; Sinha, 1956, 1962). However, a full picture of Dutch slave trade in and from Bengal with South Africa as the target is not yet available.

Chapter four of the first volume of Narendra Krishna Sinha's pioneering economic history of Bengal (1956) deals with Dutch commerce in Bengal, but there is no reference to slave trade for which the Dutch were responsible. Similarly, Ashin Das Gupta's detailed study of Indian merchants in the eighteenth century (1979) makes no reference to slavery and slave trade. Tapan Raychaudhuri's research (1962) on trading activities of the Dutch East India Company in the Coromandel Coast during the seventeenth century makes several references to Dutch slave trade in Bengal, viewed from the perspective of Dutch factors in the Coromandel Coast. Thus, in 1644, the number of slaves procured from Bengal, according to Raychaudhuri, was 58. Significantly, this took place before the establishment of the Dutch garrison in the Cape. In official circles, one often heard of the rich sources of slaves in Arakan and Bengal at that time, but we do not know how successfully these were tapped in practice. In any case, a complete account of such operations is yet to be written. Here, the reference of course is to the outcome of Dutch operations from the Coromandel Coast. We would have benefited from a full picture of the operations perceived from Dutch settlements in Bengal.

The 'kantoor' (office) of Bengal was administered by a 'directeur' in council based in Chinsura, near Hooghly. Although the VOC first explored the region in 1607, the Company settled down at Hooghly only in 1635 with the establishment of a factory, after receiving permission from the Mughals who were the reigning authorities in the region. Other trading posts established in the region were Cossimbazar (West Bengal), Patna and Rajmahal (Bihar), Balasore (Orissa), and Dhaka (modern-day Bangladesh). The factories in Bengal were managed from the 'kantoor' of the Coromandel Coast until 1655. The British finally took over the control of the settlements after 1825. Bengal's main commodities of trade were silk and other textiles, opium, and saltpetre. Significantly, slaves were hardly mentioned at that time in official documents.

It is to be noted that recently, working on alternative sources, Markus Vink has come to the conclusion that every year, between 1626 and 1662, the Dutch exported with 'reasonable regularity' 150-400 slaves from 'the Arakan-Bengal coast' and that the earliest slaves of the Cape were mainly from Bengal. It is generally held that this practice came to a stop after Bengal had been incorporated into the Mughal empire.

Bengal's contribution to regional trade during this period has been studied; but on the face of it, slaves did not account for much in such operations. Om Prakash's detailed research (1985) on the activities of the VOC in Bengal from 1630 to 1720 speaks of the important role played by Bengal in the Euro-Asian and intra-Asian trade controlled by the Dutch. But his narrative shows that textiles, above all silk, constituted the most important commodity of export from Bengal, while the other items were rice, oil and butter, sugar, saltpeter that was exported only to Europe, and to some extent, opium. It is to be granted that Om Prakash makes a few references to the export of Bengali slaves under Dutch initiative, but those were taken to work in Dutch colonies in Indonesia.

At that time, the limited trade with Bengal was carried out from the Coromandel Coast as has been indicated above. An autonomous and separate trading post for Bengal could be established in Hooghly, only after the Mughal emperor Shahjahan had issued a *farman* (imperial decree or edict) on 1 August 1635 permitting the Dutch to trade in Bengal from there. But in 1636, the Mughal viceroy of Bengal slapped a new order, banning export of slaves and saltpeter. An imperial *farman* reversed this ban shortly after in 1638. Political developments of this nature must have affected slave trade between Bengal and other countries, including the Dutch possessions in South Africa.

Later in the second half of the seventeenth century, Bengal had a flourishing export trade with Japan and some other Asian territories; for example, the

Dutch East Indies administered from Batavia, Persia, Ceylon, Malabar, and the Coromandel Coast. Taking figures for three consecutive years, with a gap of roughly thirty years, viz. 1665-66, 1693-94, and 1720-21, we are in a position to elaborate on the dynamics of Bengal's export trade.

Table 1: Bengal's Export Trade with Major Partners (1665/66-1720/21)

	1665-66 % of total	1693-94 % of total	1720-21 % of total
Europe	45.19	77.28	76.01
Japan	40.72	6.35	4.37
Batavia	Not available	12.33	16.50
Ceylon	4.99	1.86	0.75
Persia	8.35	1.53	1.34
Rest of Asia	0.17	0.04	0.71
Coromandel Coast	0.54	0.58	0.20
Malabar	Not available	Not available	0.09

Source: Om Prakash (1985), Table 3.5, pp. 76-79.

Contemporary records do not suggest that Bengal's trade with the Cape (or even with Africa in general) was of any significance during the period. There are some references to ships plying between Bengal and the Cape, in both directions (Reference: Series TAB4969 of the years 1797-1802, Documents 167-186; Cape Town National Archives). Captains of most of the ships complained about the damage suffered by the ships and the crew due to inclement weather. A major export item in such operations was rice, which the boats carried from Bengal to the Cape and elsewhere.

Thus, studies of transoceanic trade suggest that slaves hardly played a part in export and import trade from Bengal at that time. As far as Africa is concerned, it seems that Bengali slaves who were brought to the Cape came mostly by way of Batavia. This information accords well with the accounts of that period that speak of the presence of a substantial slave population in that city (Prakash, 1985: 149).

There are contemporary records that show that inhabitants of the region covering Indonesia and Malaysia, especially Malaka, were familiar with Bengalis. We have a delightful record of probably the first European ship carrying 'Frank' traders to Malaka (contemporary Malacca). *Sejarah Melayu*[3] (*The Malay Annals*) (chapter xii) tells us that, on its arrival, curious inhabitants of Malaka thronged the port to see how the newcomers looked like. On seeing them, Malaka residents 'were all astonished and said, 'These are white Bengalis' (quoted by Subramanyam, 1990: 96). Van Leur's account (1955) of the arrival of the first Dutch boat at the town of Bantam in 1596, based on contemporary documents, narrates how local people plus resident foreigners came to see the boat. 'There came such a multitude of Javanese and other nations as Turks, Chinese, Bengali, Arabs, Persians, Gujarati and others that one could hardly move' (Van Leur, 1955: 3).

*** Early Bengali enslavement

Clearly, what is said above applies to Bengal's trade during the period of Dutch hegemony in the Indian Ocean. There is evidence that prior to that period, some trade involving Bengali slaves was carried out when the Portuguese were the most powerful maritime nation in the area. Contemporary records speak of Portuguese freebooters, aided and abetted by Arakanese and Moghmarauders, mounting attacks on defenceless villagers in the delta of south Bengal and capturing men, women, and children indiscriminately to be sold as slaves in Arakan (Arasaratnam, S. [1995] 'Slave Trade in the Indian Ocean' in Mathew, K. S. [Ed.]. *Mariners, Merchants and Oceans*. New Delhi). This point has been discussed in greater detail in the section on Asian sources of data used in the present monograph.

There are other documents of that period that speak of the prevalence of the transoceanic trade and its accompanying brutalities involving adventurers other than the Dutch. In 1526, a ship from Bengal was captured by a Portuguese captain on the Coromandel Coast on the grounds that the ship carried no pass that had to be issued customarily by the Portuguese at that time, and the goods and merchandise of the ship were sold on board. The 'merchandise' included six Bengali eunuchs. The record adds nonchalantly that the captain also sold the Muslim *nakhuda* (commander) and his family into slavery (Subramanyam, 1990: 122).

All contemporary accounts agree that there were three regions of the Indian subcontinent, viz. Arakan and Bengal, Malabar, and the Coromandel Coast, that proved to be the most fertile sources of forced labor migration during this period. Vink's reference to the annual export of 150-400 slaves from the Arakan-Bengal coast by the Dutch may justifiably suggest that in the early part of Batavia's history, slaves from these three areas accounted for a considerable part of the labour force of the Company's Asian headquarters that could already claim a large slave population. Not surprisingly, between 1646 and 1649, 126 (59.71%) of the 211 manumitted slaves in Batavia originated from South Asia. Of them, 86 (a little less than 50%) were from Bengal (Vink, 2008: 5).

There were other actors too in the drama. According to some, a considerable number of Bengali slaves were brought to the Cape by British traders in the first half of the eighteenth century (Worden, 1985: 48). Aniruddha Ray's study (1998) of Bengal from around 1575 to circa 1715 mentions flourishing trade in horses, textiles, spices, rice, and sugar. Although there is no reference to slave trade on a large scale, Ray reports that at the beginning of the eighteenth century, there was an unconfirmed allegation that the English were making slaves of local Muslims and exporting forty such slaves monthly to England (Ray, 1998: 183). There is no clear information as to how far it is true and, if true, how long this continued. Om Prakash, quoting from a contemporary Danish source, has alluded to the possible involvement of Danes in this business. Susil Chaudhuri's research on the activities of the English East India Company in Bengal during the same period points to the role of the English company in transoceanic slave trade, although it makes no mention of the export of Bengali slaves.

On the basis of available data, we are thus led to the tentative conclusion that Dutch export of slaves to South Africa directly from Bengal did not assume substantial proportions, especially when we remember the extent and duration of such trade between the Cape on the one hand and Angola, Madagascar, and Mozambique in Africa and Batavia in south-east Asia on the other. Yet there are some contemporary records about slaves in the Cape who are described as having been brought from Bengal, either directly or via Batavia, which was the headquarter of the VOC, to the vast region of Asia, including Japan, where the Dutch carried on trade.

The absence of direct importation of Bengali slaves to the Cape agrees with the records of Dutch-Asian shipping between Bengal and the Cape. From 1665 to 1793, Dutch ships made, on a rough count, 165 voyages from Bengal 'homeward' to the Netherlands. For five of them, the Cape was not on regular stopping list. Eight of them were shipwrecked before reaching the Cape. One was captured by the English. There was no further information about them; probably they were given up as lost. Thus, in all, Dutch ships from Bengal touched the Cape 148 times on homebound voyages during this

21

period—coinciding approximately with the heyday of the transoceanic slave trade across the Indian Ocean.

The year 1795 marked the end of regular seafaring under the auspices of the VOC between the Netherlands and Asia. Early in the year, the Netherlands became involved in war with England. The last outward voyage of a VOC ship from the Netherlands took place on 26 December 1794, while the last homeward voyage of a VOC ship happened in the spring of 1795. The VOC itself was disbanded in 1798. (*Dutch-Asiatic Shipping*, voyages: 7856.4 and 7861.2. <*http://www.inghist.nl/Onderzoek/Projecten/DAS*>.

Archival papers contain no specific reference to official imports of Bengali slaves directly from Bengal except one significant instance in which the governing council at the Cape resolved, at their meeting on 16 April 1771, to ask the VOC authorities in Bengal to send slaves for its use. The Cape VOC administration probably took advantage of the tragic Bengal famine of 1769-70, in which ten millions were feared to have died.

The resolution read *inter alia*:

> And whereas because of the considerable mortality, for several consecutive years, among the Hon. Company's slaves here, there have been successive voyages from here to the island Madagascar for the trading of slaves, often with very poor results, our lack of the aforementioned useful people continues; therefore on the proposal of the Hon. Governor, [it is] approved and decided to petition for, by the requisition of our requirements from Bengal for the following year 1772, a *total of one hundred half-grown [i.e., young] slaves*, on the presupposition that they, due to the great lack of foodstuffs there, will be available at a reasonable price; therefore the Hon. Company's officials there not only will be cordially requested, to allow the same, but herewith also be notified that they will thereby do much for the Hon. Company's service, and our particular pleasure. (Emphasis added)

<16 April, 1771. C149, pp. 160-68 http://databases.tanap.net/cgh>

There is reason to believe that this request was acceded to. Next year, two ships, *Lands Welvaren* and *Ijsselmonde*, brought a small number of slaves directly from Bengal to the Cape. It is well to remember that by modern standards, these boats were small with tonnage of 880 each. Consequently, the number of slaves they carried to the Cape could not have been large. Indeed, passengers from each ship who went from board at the Cape came to only five. The small number of slaves dispatched from Bengal is also in accord with the record of deaths of VOC Lodge slaves in the following period, showing only a handful of deaths of Bengali slaves.

A complete list of Bengali slaves in the Cape from 1652 to 1834 when slavery was abolished throughout the British Empire is not available. However, we have glimpses of the size of Bengali slave population in different settlements at various times.

Böeseken's archival research gives us some information about Bengali slaves during the second half of the seventeenth century. Addendum 2 of his book, quoted below, presents a list of 1,470 transactions pertaining to slaves during the period 1658-1700. Of these, 175 deal with a sale of Bengali slaves. Again, a stray inventory at the estate of Johanna Snijman of Drooge Valleij farm prepared on 26 May 1755 listed thirty male and three female slaves. Of them, twelve male and one female were recorded as Bengali (Worden et al., 1996: 16). More imposing evidence comes from Nigel Worden's earlier study (1985: 47), which includes a composite list of slaves, categorised by regions of origin as recorded in the Stellenbosch district inventories of the eighteenth century. Table 4.1 of the study titled *Percentage Distribution of Slaves by Origin Recorded in Stellenbosch District Inventories* shows that Bengal's share of male slaves in Stellenbosch between 1722 and 1799 varied from 5.5 per cent in 1760-69, the lowest proportion, to 14.9 per cent in 1790-99, the highest.

Allow me to add to all this the findings of my visit to South Africa in 2002-03 during which I carried out a personal investigation at the slave quarters in Vergelegen Estate, near Somerset West. At that time, the Vergelegen museum was making a public display of some of the findings of the excavation of the old slave quarters that archaeologists had conducted shortly before. The display showed that between 1699 and 1707, Willem Adriaen van der Stel, son of Simon van der Stel, one time VOC commander of the Cape, maintained 150 slaves at the lodge whom he had purchased. The personal details of the slaves provided in the display indicated that thirteen of them were originally from Bengal.

Thus, notwithstanding the absence of exact figures, it is not impossible that in the early part of the eighteenth century, a high proportion, possibly about four-fifths according to some, of the Cape's imported slaves were from the Indian subcontinent. The percentage dropped to a little over fifteen towards the close of the authorised transoceanic slave trade (Shell, 1994: 43). That

Bengal accounted for a large proportion of these is generally accepted. It is also to be granted that the subcontinent, including Bengal, suffered a noticeable fall in its share with effect from 1760.

Finally, may I stress that in any attempt to reconstruct the history of forced Indian migration to Africa, the need to supplement the South African and Dutch sources with what may be available in India and other Asian countries can hardly be overemphasised. A conclusive account can be prepared only when all the sources have been exploited. A major feature of such an account should throw light on the participants in the slave trade, viz., the role of the VOC, how far other agencies and European powers were involved, and the extent to which private individuals—merchant adventurers, pirates, and mercenaries—contributed to the slave trade.

This book is heavily indebted to information available in South Africa, in so far as it is based, largely, on materials gathered, during 2002-03, in the National Archives of Cape Town and the libraries of the University of Cape Town, the University of Witwatersrand, and the Municipality of Cape Town. Additional data were collected through interviews with researchers working on slave trade and slavery in South Africa and with a number of South Africans, including several of those who claim descent from Bengali slaves. This book has also gained from research in Bengal, depending mainly on written materials. The author is aware that considerable amount of data is available in various archives in India, including Bengal, Chennai, Bangladesh, and Myanmar.

CHAPTER 3

Early Beginning

→ spin-off from Batavia

The materials that are accessible in the archives of South Africa shed considerable light on how the whole process of forced migration from the subcontinent and elsewhere started and continued. Robert C.-H. Shell, one of the most prolific writers on the subject, has argued justifiably that, from the outset of Dutch occupation, the Cape was a slave society. Barely a month after the Dutch settlement in 1652, Jan Antonisz van Riebeeck, founder and the first commander of the Dutch garrison at the Cape, requested the directors of the VOC to allow him to import slaves from other countries and to export the local Khoi people as slaves to the East.

Van Riebeeck could perhaps claim that his request had precedents. Slave labour was initiated in nutmeg plantations in Ambonia (Indonesia) as early as the seventeenth century. Other VOC settlements in the East Indies witnessed the introduction of the same system between 1619 and 1629. However, Van Riebeeck's proposal was rejected by the VOC.

stow away

In the event, the first imported slave Abraham van Batavia, originally from Batavia, arrived at the Cape in 1653. The first group of slaves came in 1658 from the Guinea Coast. A second lot arrived soon from Angola. The number of slaves in the Cape grew steadily. According to Boxer, the Cape had only around 800 adult slaves at the start of the eighteenth century, but the number swelled to about 4,000 fifty years later and to some 10,000 in 1780 (1965: 259). Worden et al. (1996: 43) have worked out the growth of the slave and burgher populations in the Cape. Tables 2 and 3 are taken from his book.

Table 2: Male and Female Slaves in the Cape (1726-1834)

Year	Males	Females	Total
1726	2,992	708	3,700
1770	6,198	1,906	8,104
1806	19,346	10,515	29,861
1825	19,063	13,767	32,830
1834	19,580	16,589	36,169

French/
Mozambican
slave traffic

Table 3: Adults and Children in Slave and Burgher Population in the Cape (1726-1825)

	Slaves		Burghers	
	Adults	Children	Adults	Children
1726	3,326	374	1,204	1,339
1770	7.187	917	3,633	4,316
1806	22,631	7,230	12,152	14,407
1825	21,008	11,822	23,075	27,352

Forced migration from the Indian subcontinent did not lag far behind. We have traced the first reference to a Bengali (manumitted) slave back to 1656, that is, four years after the foundation of the Dutch fort at the Cape, when Jan Woutersz, a soldier in the service of the VOC, married Catharina Anthonis, who hailed from Zalegon in Bengal. In the Company Resolution of 26 April 1656, Catharina was called *de eerbare Jongedochter* (in English, 'the honourable maiden') Catharina Anthonis (quoted by Böeseken, 1977: 78). However, there remains some confusion about her exact status because in the following year, Jan van Riebeeck referred in the resolution of 1657 to Woutersz as a soldier who had married the *slave* woman of Heer Bogaard. In a recent publication, Karel Schoeman mentions another mixed marriage that is said to have taken place in the same year, 1656, between a Dutch junior officer, Anthoni Muller, and a woman from Bengal called Domingo Elvingh. Nothing more is known about this marriage; it was not even recorded in Jan van Riebeeck's journal (Schoeman, 2007: 43-44).

Slightly later, Jan van Riebeeck recorded in the entry of his *daghregister* (journal) dated 6 July 1658 the public notification for the intended marriage (*banns*) between Jan Sacharias, a Dutch burgher, and Maria *van Bengale*. Maria was a slave originally from Bengal but was 'brought into freedom by the said Sacharias for this purpose'. Permission was given to the marriage as Maria understood and spoke the '*Nederduitsche tael*' (Dutch) and had 'a fair knowledge of Christ according to the reformed religion'. The last condition referred to the teachings of the Dutch Reformed Church based on the doctrines of John Calvin that was also known as *Gereformeerde Kerk* and later as *Hervormde Kerk*. This was the only Christian organisation permitted to operate in areas administered by the VOC in those days. A second entry announcing the solemnisation of the marriage on 21 July 1658 duly followed fifteen days later (van Riebeeck, *Journal*, Vol. 2, 1954: 303 and 315).

There were other, often stray, references to Bengali slaves in the decades immediately after. In Leon Hattingh's (1982) list of 151 slaves whose origins were known and who were sold between 1658 and 1700 in the Cape, as many as 26 were from Bengal. Clearly, there were fluctuations in the import of Bengali slaves. Shell points out that in 1771 abut 100 Bengali slaves came 'with a new language . . . and their new looks must have startled' local slaves (1994: 203).

Then there is the slave list for the period of 1699-1707 maintained at the Vergelegen slave lodge, a farm owned by Wilhem Adriaen van der Stel. The list contained about two hundred names of slaves (together with other particulars) originating from Madagascar, all over the East Indies, India, and one or two from West Africa (Cornell, 1998-99: 276-77). A close look at the list suggests that the percentage representation of Bengal, in its wider sense, was substantial.

CHAPTER 4

Bengali Slaves? Who Were They?

Early Dutch administration of the Cape did not have a foolproof system for the categorisation of slaves by origin. This made it difficult for historians to prepare a comparative ethnic map of the subordinate strata of Cape society. Slaves from Bengal suffered from certain additional difficulties in this respect. Very few of them were transported to the Cape directly from Bengal. Fewer still were brought in large groups. An indeterminate number came in trickles, illegally or at best semi-legally.

The problem of arriving at a definite figure of Bengali slaves in the Cape arises in part from the difficulty of identifying them. Possibly the differences in the physical features among Asian slaves such as Javanese, Balinese, Bengali, Coromandelian, Malabari, and Ceylonese (Sri Lankan) did not appear too distinctive to Europeans—officials as well as individual traders and mercenaries. Accordingly, European slave traders and owners alike found it hard to identify their precise origin just by appearance.

Additionally, a certain amount of laxity prevailed in information collection, which of course posed a problem for the identification of slaves in general. For instance, Frans of Bengal was often confused with François of Ceylon in official records. Documents of the late seventeenth century refer to several women as 'Lijsbeth van die Kaap' in the Cape. According to Böeseken ('Wie was die Vader van Lijsbeth van die Kaap?' in *Kronos*), one of the Lijsbeths was also known as 'Lijsbeth van Bengale'. Similarly, Langham-Carter (1985: 11) quoting from the Cape Archives speaks of one 'Sanchagrun' in Protea (Bishopscourt) and describes him as a Bengali on one page and a Malabari on another. To confound the matter, often the same name had different spellings. The well-known Bengali freed slave—the '*mooi*' (pretty)—Angela van Bengalen was in various documents mentioned as 'Angila', 'Ansiela', 'Anselaar', 'Ansla', and 'Hansela'.

Sometimes, the same person described himself or herself in different ways in different contexts. Alternative names of Anthonij van Bengalen were Anthonij de Later, Anthonij de Later van Japan, and Anthonij de Chinees. Occasionally, he is known to have signed his name also as Anthonij de Later van Yap(an) (Schoeman, 2007: 309).

Dutch authorities usually added the words '*van Bengal*' or '*van Bengalen*' when a slave was acquired from the territory known as Bengal at that time; but this did not necessarily establish the ethnic origin of the person concerned. In fact, depending on the context, the word 'Bengal' could, at that time, mean both the province of Bengal properly inhabited by Bengali-speaking people and the administrative region of Bengal that included, at that time, Orissa and Bihar. Some historians even went further and used the phrase 'the coast of Coromandel' or simply 'the Coast' to include Bengal (Bradlow and Cairns: 89).

Besides, archival records were prepared by various local administrators who often used different spellings for what counted generally as Bengal. In records of the *Resolutions of the Council of Policy of Cape of Good Hope*, I found as many as fifteen different words used as nouns or adjectives related to Bengal: *Bengaalel, Bengaalen, Bengaals, Bengaalsch, Bengaalsche, Bengaalse, Bengaalsen, Bengaalsse, Bengaels, Bengaelse, Bengale, Bengalen, Bengalle, Bengals, and Bengelan.*

An appropriate example of the confusion comes from the conflicting stories of the origin of Imam Achmat of Bengal who might have been a voluntary immigrant. Although Achmat is generally identified with Bengal, he was at his death described as the 'high priest of the Malays'. The confusion is cleared when we read carefully the evidence Achmat himself gave in 1825 before the Royal Commission to report on the 'native' inhabitants of southern Africa (popularly known as the Colebrooke and Bigge Commission[4]). Achmat made a statement to the effect that he was born in the Dutch settlement of Chinsura in Bengal but was of Malay extraction (Bradlow and Cairns, 1978: 20, quoting from the report of the Commission). Probably for Dutch slave dealers, the ethnic origin did not mean much; the more important issue was the place where the slave in question was acquired that would signify the regime (and law) under which the person lived before enslavement.

Distinguishing slaves' ethnic identities by toponyms, i.e. with reference to the tag of *van* followed by the name of the town or country or region where the slave was acquired, was useful for the first-generation slaves but did not help identify later generations. This is because slave children of later generations were known by their own places of birth. A Bengali slave child born in Cape Town, for example, would normally carry the name 'so-and-so *van die Kaap*'. This was manifestly brought out in many legal documents. Thus, a notarial protocol, regarding a deed of transfer in 1799, announced the transfer of 'the slave Sophie of Bengal and her two children, Louis and Rebecca, both of the Cape'. A similar document in 1801 pronounced the sale of 'Samieta of Bengal and her child Regina of the Cape'.

The problem of identification is further complicated by the fact that often a new name was given when a slave was baptised. The same thing happened at the time of manumission. Such occasions paved the way for multiple counting and also contributed to the difficulty of estimating the precise size of Bengali slaves.

On the other hand, a factor that tended to bring down the recorded number of slaves in general (including Bengali slaves) was the practice of registering new slaves under the names of dead slaves. This was possible because slaves who died were not usually struck off the registers. Robert Shell called the new slaves taking the names and identities of deceased slaves 'zombie slaves' (1994: 34).

Undercounting also took place because now and then slaves were brought to the Cape in small numbers and semi-legally as the personal cargo belonging to sailors and officials on VOC ships (Ross, 1983: 13). Moreover, on other occasions, Company officials were suspected of having deliberately understated their slave holdings given that they were not allowed to keep more than a small number of domestic slaves.

Problems of enumeration notwithstanding, there are reasons to believe that Bengali slaves constituted a substantial proportion of the total slave population in the Cape. Frank R. Bradlow and Margaret Cairns estimated that the number of slaves and free blacks from India represented more than half of the total slave population there and that those from the Coromandel Coast and Bengal together formed 42.1 per cent of the total Indian immigrants (1978: 103). Shell drew a dynamic picture of the Bengali slave population in the Cape. 'The slave trade to the Cape started in West Africa, turned east after 1706, and finally became re-Africanised after 1780' (1994: 65). He was more explicit about slaves from the Indian subcontinent. 'In the early decades of the eighteenth century, nearly 80 per cent of all slaves imported (in the Cape)

 # Shell's claims

came from the Indian subcontinent'—a statement that has been questioned by some later observers. Shell added that the proportion of slaves from the Indian subcontinent 'dropped to a little more than 15 percent in the last decades of the legal oceanic slave trade' (1994: 43).

The present author has prepared a list of more than 700 Bengali slaves and over 50 Bengali slave owners in the Cape (including Cape Town and nearby settlements and farms such as Stellenbosch, Vergelegen, and Constantia) during the period of 1652-1834 (see Appendix C of the present monograph). The list was prepared using documents from the Cape Town archives; historical materials from Stellenbosch, Vergelegen slave lodge, and Constantia; certain relevant databases available on the Internet (Cf. *Subsection D of Sources*); inventories prepared by Böeseken, Heese, Hattingh, Shell, and Worden; and some VOC documents made accessible to the public by TANAP. Other sources of the list are the transactions involving Bengali slaves during the period of 1652-1880 and the documents pertaining to both civil and criminal cases in which Bengali slaves were involved. Records of these are available in the archives of Cape Town under codes MOOC/TAB 496-, CJ/TAB 496-, and NCD/TAB 496-, among others. Understandably, several slaves and slave owners may have been counted more than once, according to the number of occasions when they were mentioned in official documents as a result of their sale, resale, manumission, and more than one involvement in legal disputes. On the other hand, some undercounting was inevitable because not all persons brought to the Cape from Bengal through extra-legal and illegal channels were registered.

It should be remembered that the names listed here refer only to first-generation slaves and slave owners of Bengali origin who could be identified, courtesy to the then prevailing practice of toponymic naming. Descendants of first-generation slaves were branded with reference to where they were born (e.g. so-and-so of the Cape or so-and-so of Batavia) or, rather, obtained from.

Place names apart, slaves were often given biblical names. Names from Greek and Roman myths and legends such as Hercules and Cupid were also given, probably because slave owners were more familiar with them. Sometimes, the name of the month or the day when a slave was acquired (viz. January, February, March, April, July, September, October, and November from month names; and Friday and Sunday from day names) was allocated to him or her. This practice was probably related to the seasonal timetable of slave-carrying boats. Even then a few native Bengali names can be found in various documents, e.g.

Malati (Malatie) (1800), Canai (Kanai) (1800), Robi (Ruby) (1801), Mina (1798), and Manika (1730) mentioned by Worden (1985: 95).

Robert Shell has classified slave names into eleven categories. These names are given below. The figures after the labels of categories refer to their frequency in the sample.

Day 0.8%; Protestant 31%; Catholic 0.4%; Old Testament 12.6%; Indigenous 10.1%; Muslim 0.5%; Classical 24.8%; Month 4.3%; Facetious 5.9%; Toponyms 0.3%; and Unknown 9.25%

('Cape Slave Naming Pattern', Shell, 1994)

For comparison with our focus, the present author wished to take a random sample of slave names from the first five pages of the Bengali slave database (see appendix C at the end of this book) prepared by him and classify the names of the entries in terms of the above categories. But the idea was given up because it was soon realised that the incidence of certain day names and month names do not occur consistently at the same rate. The presence of certain day names (Tuesday and Thursday) beginning with 'T' and certain other names (Sunday and Saturday) beginning with 'S' will vitiate the process of selecting a 'random' sample from the whole list. The same remark applies to month names. However, taking all names under 'S' which includes Sunday and Saturday as day names and September as a month name, the following results were obtained.

Total names in the inventory beginning with 'S' = 35

Day 0%; Protestant 31%; Catholic 0.4%; Old Testament 12.6%; Indigenous 10.1%; Moslem 0.5%; Classical 24.8%; Month 8.0%; Facetious 5.9%; Toponyms 0.3%; and Unknown 9.25%

It is tempting to discover a deeper motive behind the practice of renaming newly acquired slaves. Giving a slave a new name meant creating a fresh identity for him or her in a new society and would tend to suppress his or her traditional roots. This practice, in different contexts, prevails in many societies. Adopting a new name on conversion to a new religion is pervasive. Within the same religious community, a new name is usually given when a religious neophyte is initiated as a member of the higher-status clergy. A comparable ritual prevails in many monarchical systems when, on being crowned, a fresh incumbent of the throne assumes a new title, often after a previous holder of the post, perhaps to shine in his/her reflected glory. In all these cases, the idea presumably is to demolish all associations of the past and mark the inauguration of a new life.

Yet, this thesis, attractive although it is, cannot be accepted at its face value. Toponymic names are common in many societies, including some parts of India. In the Cape itself, the practice was applied additionally to white or European officials of VOC. Even some of the top Company officials were named in the same manner. Thus, a leading governor of the Cape was referred to as Simon van der Stel of Mauritius; other names of this type were Jan Sacharias from Amsterdam and Jan Roeloffszoon van Copenhagen. There is a difference though. A toponymic label in the case of a European does not entirely wipe out her or his previous identities. Simon van der Stel and other persons in a comparable situation had several other identification marks from their previous lives. There was no need to suppress them. On the contrary, bearers of such marks took pride of them. Slaves in the Cape found themselves in a very different situation.

CHAPTER 5

Bengali Slave Owners

Interestingly, even during the early years of Dutch rule in the Cape, lists prepared by historians mention at least a dozen Bengali slave owners, branded variously as 'black slave owners', 'black farmers', and 'free blacks' (*vryswart*).[5] A list of Bengali slave owners compiled from different sources by the present author consists of forty-eight Bengali slave owners between the mid-seventeenth century and the mid-nineteenth century (see Appendix D). This issue has been subjected to a more detailed analysis in the sections entitled *Endnotes* and *Sources*.

The first mention of a Bengali slave owner (Anthoni) is found in a record of 1676, just twenty-four years after the establishment of the Cape garrison. Anthoni is variously described as *vrij ingesetene alhier* ('free local resident') and a *'free burgher'*, who, according to Böeseken, sold a slave from Bali – Baddou – to Governor Bax at Rds 50. Two years later, a slave dealer, Paul, sold Aletta Hinlopen to Anthoni for Rds 100.

Another list compiled by Hattingh (1982), who teaches at the University of the Western Cape, contains the names of at least three Bengali slave purchasers, viz. Domingo of Bengal, Anthony of Bengal, and Louis of Bengal. Louis of Bengal acquired a slave in 1687 called 'Matthijs Java', aged twenty-seven. The name suggests that Matthijs was from the island of Java, in present-day Indonesia. However, in all likelihood, he was not Javanese, ethnically speaking that is, because enslavement of the Javanese and the Balinese, as well as Amerindians and Khoisan[6] (the so-called 'Hottentots' and 'Bushmen'), was strictly forbidden in Dutch territories by the *Heeren XVII*[7] (in English, 'the

Gentlemen Seventeen'), directors of VOC. Andrew Bank (1991: 236-37) prepared yet another list of 'free black slave owners' in Cape Town and Cape District for his MA thesis in the early 1990s. The list identified the ethnicity of free black slave owners numbering 131, of whom 15 were originally from Bengal. Altogether they owned 44 slaves. The three largest groups of slave owners were from the Cape (47.34%), Bengal (11.45%), and Batavia (9.92%). The breakdown of slave owners by country of origin is shown in Appendix C.

Table 4: Free Black Slave Owners in Cape Town and Cape District (1816-34)

Countries of origin	Absolute number	% of total
1. The Cape	62	47.34
2. Bengal	15	11.45
3. Batavia	13	9.92
4. Bougies	8	
5. Ceylon	5	
6. Macassar	4	
7. Mauritius	2	
8. Pondichery	2	
9. Java	2	
10. Madagascar	1	
11. Bali	1	
12. Malacca	1	
13. Ambon	1	
14. Mozambique	1	
15. Others (Sama rang, Franquebar, Westkust, etc.)	8	
16. Origin unknown	5	
Total	131	

Various accounts show that several freed Bengali slaves did well in later life. Perhaps the most well known is Angela *van Bengalen*. Angela's early life is shrouded in mystery. Her later life in captivity is better known. It is reported that in the late 1650s, Pieter Kemp, a 'free burgher' of Batavia, brought Angela together with her husband or consort and three children to the Cape and sold them to Jan van Riebeeck. At that time, van Riebeeck was the governor of the Cape. In 1662, van Riebeeck sold the family to Abraham Gabbema. When Gabbema was transferred to Batavia in 1666, he set Angela and her three children free. What happened to the husband (or partner) is unknown, but in 1669, Angela married the free burgher Arnoldus Willemsz from Wesel later known as Arnoldus Willemsz Basson.

Several historians, including H. F. Heese (1981: 39), have provided details of Angela's marriage with Basson in 1669 and her life thereafter. The husband died in 1698, but Angela lived for another twenty-two years. Considering her background marked by multiple deprivations, Angela's rise in the social hierarchy of the Cape was nothing less than spectacular. Apparently, she was an illiterate woman from a family in Bengal who was sold as a slave to a Portuguese buccaneer. She was brought to a strange land, the Cape, as a slave, and was sold to the Dutch commander of the garrison. In Cape society, she must have suffered because of her skin colour. To cap it all, in the highly patriarchal milieu of Burgher society, Angela must have faced gender discrimination in terms of reproductive exploitation (child-bearing function and the socialisation of the child), sexual exploitation involving the illicit use of the body, and gender exploitation amounting to the general abuse of the status of women, common to all women in most societies. Despite all these, Angela outshone many other slaves, less disadvantaged than her.

Towards the end of her life when her children had married and moved to settle elsewhere, Angela lived in her garden house in Table Valley until 1720 when she died. Angela has been described as a 'tough business-woman, wine-maker, brandy distiller and market-gardener' (Malan, 1998-99: 64-65). She had three male and two female slaves living with her. There is no way to fix the identity of the women, but the men were from India: the (Coromandel) 'coast', Malabar, and Bengal (Malan, 1998-99).

Slightly later than Angela, there are many references to Louis van Bengale, described as 'a colourful character' ('*n kleurryke figuur*') of the period. He came to the Cape as a slave in 1664; he gained freedom from slavery reportedly in 1673 and was baptised in 1675. Eventually, he himself became a slave owner. Louis was one of the first free blacks to employ white *knecht*s or slave supervisors. He is known to have employed Willem Teerling, a white *knecht*. More interestingly, he is reported to have sacked Teerling, an act of considerable courage for a former black slave living on the periphery of a white society. Louis owned much landed property, including the Lanzerac farm, later a fashionable Stellenbosch hotel. J. L. Hattingh (1981: 21) has provided details of his fortune as well as those of his progeny through several wives and mistresses (*Kronos* 3, 1980).

An exercise in terms of two parameters, age and gender, was attempted for slave owners of Bengali origin using the data of Tables 5 and 6. Here the category 'age' is not particularly relevant, as slave owners were all, understandably, adult. The high proportion of men (around 72 per cent) among slave owners is not surprising; on the contrary, what is of importance is that more than 28 per cent of Bengali slave owners should be women! As mentioned above, Angela van Bengale, perhaps the earliest Bengali female slave owner, was a formidable business woman who had three male and two female slaves living with her in a garden house in Table Valley. One of the three male slaves is known to have been from Bengal. Angela might have had other Bengali slaves elsewhere.

A flashier picture comes into view from the records of Anna de Koning, Angela's daughter. Ironically, Anna, though herself being a descendant of a former slave from an unknown father, married a Swedish officer in the service of VOC, Captain Oloff Bergh, in 1678. At the death of her husband, Anna inherited and managed for ten years until her death in 1734 a huge estate and winery, *Groot Constantia* ('Big Constantia'), near Cape Town, and other substantial properties and assets. Anna owned twenty-eight slaves in her several houses in town, seven in her garden and farms in Table Valley, and twenty-seven at her prize farm, *Groot Constantia*, a total of sixty-two! Paradoxically, one of these was from Bengal (1997: 19).

Slavery was made illegal in British territories in 1834, which is why the last record of Bengali slave owners can be found in that year. As many as fifteen Bengali slave owners (out of a total of thirty-nine) are listed in that year. Altogether, they possessed a total of forty-two slaves. Judging by the number of slaves owned, the richest Bengali slave owner in that year was David, who owned 10 slaves.

The upward mobility of some of the former Bengali slaves is striking. At the time of manumission, probably none of them had any capital. Most of them took to selling grocery provisions, fishing, and catering. Apparently all of them started their new lives in hardship and, at least in the beginning, found it difficult to own land. Despite all these disadvantages, some of them attained great heights of prosperity.

In an interesting paper, Gerald Groenewald (2006) has shown how 'human capital' (natural talents, acquired skills, and personal experiences) combined with 'social capital' (the size and scope of a person's social network consisting of his family and friends and his ability to make use of the resources at the disposal of the latter) helped mid-eighteenth-century entrepreneurs dealing in alcohol to flourish. Application of this framework to trace the social mobility of Bengali slave owners may result in a fascinating study.

References have already been made to Angela of Bengal and her daughter Anna de Koning as examples of the success of freed Bengali slaves. Among other affluent Bengali slave owners was Robert Schott (alternative spelling Robert Schot) of Bengal who possessed eight slaves at the time of his death in 1741. In addition, he owned a farm, Koornhoop on the Liesbeeck River, a market garden, `tsche Kloof in Cape Town, and other pieces of landed property (Shell: 262-63 and Randle: 19-20). His estate inventory also included a number of gold and silver items, expensive linen, and some ivory combs. He enjoyed his status as landlord; he was rich enough to operate as a money lender into the bargain.

Among others were Louis of Bengal, David, who possessed ten slaves, listed in Bank's slavery inventory of 1833, and, Achilles, a tallow chandelier listed in Bank's slavery inventory and having six slaves. February, Jack—a retailer, and Lakey were listed in Bank's slavery inventory and possessed four slaves each.

Prosperity of Bengali slave owners is not to be measured solely by the number of slaves owned. There were other measures as well. Jacob van Bengalen employed a private tutor to further his children's education (Faasen in TEPC 2006: 18). The case of Louis of Bengal who employed a white man, William Teerling, as a knecht to work on his farm and then summarily disposed of his service has already been mentioned. Louis also owned a classy hotel in Stellenbosch, Lanzerac.

X mooc records (estate records) indicates property owned.

An assessment of the financial position of Bengali free blacks can be obtained from a study of the inventories made of their estates after their death when these were disposed of by auctions. Such public sales were held regularly, and detailed records of these transactions are available in the archives. While slaves participated in them only as objects of sale and purchase, Bengali free blacks took part in them as sellers and buyers, either actual or potential.

In her online essay, *From Rags to Riches*, Therese Benadé itemises the household and personal belongings of Angela van Bengale that were recorded in an inventory after her death and later auctioned. Among jewellery were four gold rings, a string of pearls with matching drop earrings, many strands of beads, and an English silver watch; black ebony chairs, porcelain plates, and dishes; an oval table in the centre of the room with silver spoons and forks, butter dish, and teacups; and a framed mirror. Then there was the kitchen filled with iron and copper pots, cake pans, a waffle iron, a multitude of tin plates, scales, barrels, a brandy distiller, and three jars of rosewater.

The inventory of Anna de Koning (various spellings e.g. Coning, Conning exist), prepared after her death in May 1734, was even more impressive. It recorded three houses in Cape Town, a house and garden in Table Valley, and, of course, Constantia, a farm and winery, complete with two farmsteads on loan farms along the Piquetberg. It will be tedious to catalogue the details of Anna's other earthly possessions. Suffice it to mention the more valuable items of her jewellery, appropriately described as 'the adornments of a grand lady': gold and silver chains and rings set with diamonds and pearls (one of them displaying seven diamonds!), saffires and topaz, rubies, cat eye and, agate; gold and silver buckles; a large number of silver and ebony buttons; a small gold pocket watch; and, probably to satisfy her Christian conscience, a gold-bound hymn book. [Irony]

Yet there is no reason to suppose that Bengali free blacks were on the way to becoming a substratum of the nascent Cape bourgeoisie. For one thing, they were too few in number. Equally importantly, despite the prosperity of some of them, Bengali free blacks were separated from the burghers by a challenging cultural and social chasm. Finally in terms of wealth, they were hopelessly unequal. This comes out clearly from figures pertaining to slaves and material assets owned by the two groups.

CHAPTER 6

Slave Trade Modalities

[Explicate]

[A comprehensive history of the organisation of Dutch slave trade in Bengal is not available. Robert Ross rightly points to the possible existence of 'as-yet-little-understood network of traders including Bengali Banians, Buginese trader pirates, Chinese junk captains, Saklava king Prazeros on the Zambezi, Portuguese officials in Delagoa Bay and south to Natal, or kidnappers in South India' (Ross, 1983: 13).]

Even after thirty years since Ross made this statement, detailed information is lacking as to how slaves were acquired from Bengal, how many of them were abducted and how many were hired originally as servants to be later sold into slavery, whether they were transported directly to the Cape or taken there via Batavia, which was then the Asian headquarters of the Dutch East India Company, and how many times their ownership changed hands. A study such as this should additionally shed light on slaves' lives in bondage, the process of manumission, and its aftermath. A full account of the organisation of Dutch slave trade in Bengal should also describe the tie-up between indigenous and foreign participants in the slave trade, viz. the role of the VOC, how far other European Powers were involved, and the extent to which private individuals—merchant adventurers, pirates, and other mercenaries—contributed to the slave trade.

Among those who have attempted to identify local and outside actors in this high drama is Professor Om Prakash of the Delhi School of Economics. Working on the documents in the Dutch archives that include the 'shipping lists' for the ports of Hooghly and Balasore, Om Prakash (1985: 26-34) presents a 'broad structure of trade' involving Bengal. Our knowledge is partial because

(handwritten margin notes: " Shipping lists for Hoogly & Balasore")*

the shipping lists contain information only about the ship-owning merchants and not about those who took part in the trade by hiring freight space on ships owned by others. Om Prakash's account suggests that only 41 per cent of the merchants based in ports of Bengal had their domicile in Bengal. He added that about a third of them were officials of the Mughal administration, petty and high. The use (or rather the abuse) of official position to further their private interests was discouraged. However, manipulation of the power and influence by an officeholder to increase the margin of profit in private trade was common.

A large percentage of these officials were Muslim. However, private merchants who owned ships also included Hindu and Armenian (presumably Christian) traders. Muslim merchants were more numerous than their Hindu counterparts, who operated principally from the port of Balasore. Gujarati Shahs dominated this group. Among Hindu merchants, we find some typical Bengali names such as Jadu Ray and Kalyan Ray; but they accounted for a small portion of the total trade. True enough, the dominant group among Hindu merchants was composed of *bania*s; and many of them were originally from Gujarat and 'other places' (sic) (Prakash, 1985: 104). This is confirmed by other researches. Susil Chaudhuri (1975) points out that of the eighteen prominent merchants who supplied raw silk and piece-goods (principal items of export from Bengal) to the VOC in Kasimbazar in the 1680s, nine were Gujaratis. According to him, this was in sharp contrast with what happened in Surat and Madras (Chennai), where all leading merchants were local people. The business acumen and trustworthiness of the merchants operating from Bengal has been described by Commissioner van Rheede with a terse concluding comment: 'In general, they are a people with whom one could get along well so long as one is on one's guard' (quoted by Prakash, 1985: 105).

Interestingly, we know from other sources that some African traders (referred to as Abyssinian merchants) participated in this trade. *The Book of Duarte Barbosa* mentions their presence among merchants from 'other countries' in Chittagong (called by the Portuguese the '*porto grande*', i.e. 'big haven') and Gaur or Satgaon labelled as the '*porto piqueno*' (i.e. 'little haven') (Subramanyam, 1990: 118). Unfortunately, no further information about them is available.

Then there are stray references to the role played by other European powers in abducting slaves from Bengal. Quoting from a contemporary Danish source, Ole Feldbaek (1991) has alluded to the possible involvement of Danes in the piracy disguised as 'justifiable warfare', which seemingly resulted in the sale of prisoners as slaves. Around 1640, a Danish ship was stranded off the coast of Bengal near Pipli (other names: Baliapal or Piplipatan; now in Orissa). Local authorities declined, allegedly, to offer help in salvaging goods. Nor would they give up what was retrieved. Danes interpreted this refusal as 'robbery' and felt justified in retaliating. Consequently, for more than thirty years, Danish ships regularly seized boats and cargoes operating to and from Bengal. It is likely that during such operations some seized persons were sold into slavery to others, including Dutch slave traders. A painting (*Arrakanese pirates selling Bengali slaves in Pipli slave market*) exhibited in the online series <*www.atlasofmutualheritage.nl*> provides visual testimony to such practice (see Appendix G). There are additionally many references to the purchase of Bengali slaves from private individuals by the authorities of the VOC in the Cape. The story of Angela *van Bengalen* ('the *maaij* or *mooi* Ansela' or 'the pretty Angela' as she was often described in contemporary Dutch records) is a case in point.

The modus operandi of slave trade affecting Bengal should additionally be discussed from the perspective of the Cape. In the early decades following the settlement at the Cape, slave trade was the monopoly of the VOC. There were official expeditions, among other places, to Madagascar and Mozambique for the acquisition of slaves by raiding and capturing unsuspecting locals and also through purchase. All these were aimed at augmenting the slave population at the Slave Lodge (*Slaven Logie*), the slave house, the construction of which was completed by the VOC in 1679. Highly placed Company officials were not legally allowed to own slaves, but they, termed as 'patricians' by Robert Shell (1997: xxxii), possessed some. In 1658, soldiers of the VOC were given land and allowed to become 'free burghers'. Since then, many of them harboured the desire to participate in slave trade on their own. Between 1687 and 1784, burghers sent as many as five petitions to the authorities with a request to allow private initiative in the slave trade. It was only in 1791 that the slave trade was opened to private enterprise.

CHAPTER 7

Preferences for Slaves

Bengali slaves, like slaves of other ethnic groups, were acquired for different purposes. Dutch colonial authorities engaged some of them directly and kept them in the Slave Lodge in Cape Town, while free burghers purchased other slaves for help in domestic chores. Additionally, some slaves worked on farms and plantations. The Company Slave Lodge was the largest slave holding throughout the seventeenth century with more slaves than those in all other households taken together.

According to the slave traders and owners, the slaves from Madagascar were excellent at agriculture, while Angolan slaves could do very hard work. The slaves from India and some places in Indonesia were much appreciated for their abilities as craftsmen. (TANAP, *Introduction to Resolutions of the Council of Policy of the Cape of Good Hope*, Section on Slavery).

The prices typically paid for slaves from various countries indicated the operation of a kind of preferential scale for slaves of different origins (e.g. 'Creole' status denoting birth in the Cape) and of supposed criteria of 'racial' descent (e.g. 'mulatto' status denoting persons of mixed blood) with associated qualities of brain and brawn. These stereotypes were indirectly responsible for a hierarchy of preferences, leading to the fixing of different prices for slaves. The rating scale was noticed by many visitors and others who wrote on Cape society in the past.

It is well to point out that the hierarchy of preferences through different periods and as seen by various observers was not uniform. Writing towards the end of the eighteenth century, Otto Mentzel, a well-known German visitor to the Cape and named 'the Herodotus of the early Cape' by Robert Shell (1997: 457), reported that Indian, especially Bengali, female slaves were preferred for their skill in needlework (1785/1925).

Such preference was furthermore manifested in the incorporation process. Speaking of the early years of Cape slavery, Robert Shell maintained that Mulatto female slaves marrying bachelor burghers or Company employees were most frequently incorporated into the settler community. Women from the Indonesian archipelago and from India (Bengal) came next in that order [Cited by Malan (1998-99: 51)].

In the allocation of slaves to different jobs, contemporary observers have noted a kind of perceived occupational capabilities based on ethnicity. Creole slaves occupied the top position, presumably because of their local birth that lent them a measure of familiarity and stability in assigned positions. Mulatto slaves too were highly preferred, probably because of their European descent. Next in the hierarchy were slaves from Indonesia, African countries other than Madagascar, the Indian subcontinent, and Madagascar in that order (Shell, 1994: 51).

However, stereotyping was not static. It depended, among other things, on the magnitude of the supply of slaves from different regions, their mortality rate due to the propensity to falling victims to local maladies, and knowledge of their work records among potential purchasers, including involvement in crimes and reports of absenteeism and escape from the master's establishment. Moreover, it is well to remember that assessment of the usefulness of slaves was to an extent subjective, and, therefore, it was bound to vary from one observer to another.

All the same, there was general agreement on the top and the bottom layers of the hierarchy. Mulatto and Creole slaves were at the top. Increasingly, the two categories were combined. The lowest rank was generally reserved for the Malagasy slaves. The opinion about the position of slaves from Indonesia and the Indian subcontinent including Bengal varied. Female Asian slaves' skill in needlework came for special mention (cf. p.44). In several cases, Bengali slave women were praised for various other reasons. The South African Cultural History Museum in Cape Town displays a piece of lace knitted supposedly by Malati, a Bengali slave (Cornell, 1998-99, 263).

CHAPTER 8

Demographic Profile

With these cautionary remarks, we may present here a demographic profile of the first-generation slaves of Bengali origin (cf. Tables 5 and 6) and slave owners of Bengali origin in 1676–1833 (cf. Table 4).

Two points are to be emphasised in this context. First, the bimodality of the distribution of the Bengali slave population in the two periods, viz. 1652–1700 and 1751–1800, is easily seen (Table 5). The relatively high figure of slaves in the first period is explained by the desperate need for labour in the new establishment of the Cape. This agrees with Professor Shell's observation about the dynamics of Bengali slave population in the Cape as is evident in the figures in the fourth row in the table. Probably, the acquisition of a large number of slaves during 1751–1800 was necessitated by the demand for labour in an expanding plantation economy.

Table 5: First-generation Slaves of Bengali Origin by Gender and Time Periods

Years	Male	Female	Total
1652–1700	177	60	237
1701–1750	63	51	114
1751–1800	30	98	228
1801–18xx	67	34	101
Total 1652–18xx	437	243	680

Table prepared by author as detailed above.

The entries in the list were also tabulated by gender (see above) and age (where it was recorded). Table 6 sums up the findings regarding age distribution. As could be expected, the age category 16–30 accounts for about 78 per cent of all slaves. The proportion is even higher if we consider only male slaves (>79 per cent). Fourteen out of 154 slaves were below 10; these were transferred from one owner to another along with their mothers.

Table 6: The Known Profiles of Bengali Slaves by Gender and Age [8]

Age	Male	Female	Total
1–5	4	1	5
6–10	5	4	9
11–15	14	4	18
16–30	95	25	120
30–45	1	0	1
46 and above	1 ('elderly')	0	1
Total	120	34	154

Table prepared by author as detailed above.

CHAPTER 9

Conditions in Which Bengali Slaves Lived and Worked

Like slaves belonging to all other ethnic communities, Bengali slaves were subject to a stringent disciplinary code known as the *Tulbagh Code*. This was issued in 1753 by Rijk Tulbagh, governor of the Cape Colony. Under these rules, public streets were declared out of bounds for all slaves after 10 p.m. A slave was required to carry a pass and a lantern, if for any reason he had to go out. Conversation with other slaves on the streets was prohibited at all times. Riding on wagons and horses in the street was also prohibited for all slaves. During services, they were not permitted to assemble outside the entrances of church buildings.

Additional regulations that made life difficult for all slaves, including Bengali slaves, are summarised below.

- ➢ Slaves were not allowed to sing, whistle, or make any kind of sound at night. They could not enter public houses or taverns. Nor could they stop to converse on the streets of Cape Town.
- ➢ Slaves were not allowed to congregate in groups on public holidays.
- ➢ Slaves were not permitted to carry, or own, firearms.
- ➢ Slaves who made false claims against or insulted freemen were punished by public flogging and held in chains.
- ➢ Slaves committing violence against their masters were put to death.

Such disciplinary regime governed the lives of Bengali slaves and their relationship with other ethnic communities. It also impacted on their family life.

Family Life

A basic difficulty in forming a stable slave family was the sexual imbalance of the slave population. This was particularly true of the eighteenth century. Even at the end of the century, adult male slaves numbered three times more than adult female slaves in Stellenbosch; the imbalance was considerably greater in the interior (Worden, 1982: 57).

Sexual imbalance created jealousy and rivalry among male slaves for the favours of female slaves and Khoi women. This state of affairs sometimes led to violence of which Bengali slaves had their fair share. In 1797, January van Bengal stabbed his rival Moses van de Kaap and was brought to justice where January admitted that he did it out of jealousy (Worden, 1982: 57). This was not an isolated case.

Absence of stable family life was partly responsible for rape and other sexual offences. To start with, less than 1 per cent of slaves were brought to the Cape in families (Shell, 1994: 125). This is an estimate for all Cape slaves, but there is no reason to suppose that the proportion was different among Bengali slaves. On the contrary, unlike slaves of certain other regions such as those exported from Mozambique and Madagascar, many of whom were acquired in groups, Bengali slaves were transported in isolation from their kith and kin. Slaves were bought and sold individually, especially because old and sick persons had no use to slave purchasers. This is why, more often than not, slave families were split when a transfer took place.

On the other hand, some masters tried to preserve the unity of their slave families by transferring them as a whole or by bequeathing them to one person in their wills. The prime example is provided by the case of *Angela van Bengalen*, who was sold by Pieter Kemp to Jan van Riebeeck in the 1650s together with her consort (husband?) and three children. Jan van Riebeeck, the new owner of Angela, on his turn sold her together with her children and possibly also her consort to Basson, thus keeping the family united. Later accounts show that the family remained united as long as Angela was alive. But it is difficult to guess the extent to which Angela set the pattern for later transactions.

In 1782, a ban was imposed on the sale of young slave children separately from their mothers—a measure that should have contributed to the stability of the core of a slave family, viz. a mother and her children. We do not know if things improved in reality after this event. A legislation of 1823 endorsed legal marriage of slaves and ordained that slaves married according to Christian rites might not be sold separately. Unfortunately, marriage according to rites of religions other than Christianity was not legally recognised. The most aggrieved were Muslims because compared to other ethnic communities, they had a detailed system of marriage regulations formally codified with institutional backing via mosques and marriage officers.

Furthermore, Cape laws considered slaves to be 'children' of their masters, and, thus, a slave had to secure the consent of his or her master for marriage. No wonder, up to 1831, just three legal (Christian) marriages were registered when the slave population of the Cape was 35,000 (Shell, 1994: 321).

Apparently, in spite of some honourable exceptions, slave owners were not particularly interested in encouraging stable slave families. Even if they were so inclined, circumstances made it difficult for them to pursue this line consistently. Commonly, slaves who were obtained overseas were brought and sold in the Cape as individuals. Once here, some of them formed unions with other slaves. Sometimes, in the absence of slave partners, a male slave lived together with a *Khoikhoi* woman in a rural area, referring to himself as the *man* ('husband') and the woman as the *vrouw* ('wife') with considerable pride.

A key obstacle in the way of free choice in such unions was the small size of many farms and households where domestic slaves were employed. Certainly, a union, whether legal or customary, between two Bengali slaves was bound to be difficult in such circumstances. Moreover, the possibility of sale at auctions and of the consequent break of the unit hung over their transient union like the infamous sword of Damocles.

There are many references to Bengali slaves (predominantly male) contracting sexual union with slaves from other ethnic communities: slaves from Coromandel and Malabar in what today is India, Ceylonese slaves, slaves from Malay and various islands of the Indonesian archipelago, and black slaves from Madagascar and Mozambique. The cases mentioned below are only illustrative and by no means conclusive.

Louis from Bengal, one of the earliest free blacks, married Rebecca van Macassar, an Indonesian slave, with whom he lived for many years. Louis additionally contracted some kind of relationship with the Hottentottine (Khoi woman), Zara, well known at that time, although there was some controversy as to whether she was formally married to him.

In these circumstances, even the assertion and maintenance of paternal (or maternal) authority was difficult, let alone the development of a strong family tradition in which future members of the unit could genuinely take pride. How could a father exercise parental control over children when they or even his wife were objects of sexual desire of his master?

The story of Manika van Bengal, a consort of Reijnier of Madagascar, amply illustrates the point. The master of the slave couple was so infatuated by the beauty of their daughter of fourteen that his jealous wife started thrashing the young girl relentlessly. One day when the torture was particularly severe, furious Reijnier attacked and thrashed his master in revenge. He then ran away and for the next eight years remained in hiding as a fugitive, until he was captured and identified by his former partner, Manika. (Worden, 1985: 95-96)

This was not an isolated case. Sexual relationships between white free burghers and Asian and black slave women as well as legally free Khoi women ('Hottentottine') were not uncommon. On the other hand, there were some adulterous cases involving white burgher women and male slaves belonging to other ethnic groups. In 1714, a Bengali slave, named Titus of Bengal, had a love affair with his master's wife. The two lovers, abetted by several other slaves, killed their master (Worden, 1982: 59). The court condemned Titus to death. Then there is the case of Cupido (or Kupido, according to some documents) of Bengal who was alleged to have had a 'criminal conversation' (sic) with the daughter of his master. But such liaisons were not common, and in all cases, they led to severe penalties imposed on the slave. Expectedly, the sentence given to the white mistresses in such instances was much less severe, if at all it was administered.

Occupations

In Cape Town, outside the Slave Lodge, slavery was mainly domestic in nature, as far as female slaves were concerned. By and large, they were engaged in performing domestic chores: cleaning, washing, cooking, and looking after babies and children. More often than not, they lived in the same houses or at least in the vicinity of the masters' houses. The treatment meted out to them is supposed to have been milder than what slaves on farms had to endure. Mention should also be made of the use of some slaves as artisans, especially male slaves. Thus, Antonia Malan, an academic of the University of Cape Town, gave the name of Augustus of Bengal as a woodcarver in her account of the wealthy Storm family of Blettermanhuis (Cornell, 74-75). There are references to a Bengali slave trumpet blower by occupation. August of Bengal, a slave of Christiaan Daniel Perzoon, was a tailor (MOOC8/17.22, 1776). There are other references to different skills of slaves of the time. Indeed by the early nineteenth century, all artisans of the colony were slaves or former slaves. In rural areas, slaves were engaged in farming or helping in farm work. But some slaves were given the job of herding cattle or sheep. Generally, these were men's work, and commonly, slaves from Mozambique and Madagascar were preferred for such work.

Working Conditions

Harsh treatment meted out to slaves has been reported in various accounts. Apart from subjecting their slaves to physical torture and molestation, the masters often got rid of them through resale. Those convicted of crime were resold in chains. Interestingly, the sole extant eighteenth-century public announcement of a sale of this kind related to one Alexander of Bengal, aged sixteen years (Shell, 1997: 97).

Housing and Living Conditions

The quality of housing varied considerably from the Slave Lodge of the Company castle in Cape Town to houses of free burghers and rural farms. In the overcrowded Slave Lodge, the conditions in which slaves were housed are reported to have been far from sanitary. Only a minority of slaves owned by free burghers was provided with private sleeping quarters; they slept in odd places such as the attic, kitchen and outhouse of the principal residence of the masters. In general, slave women, with their children, slept apart from the men. The absence of privacy was another reason why healthy family life could not grow among the slave population.

In rural areas, some large farms provided separate sleeping quarters for slaves; however, these were sparingly furnished as evidenced by the description of the inventories of slave houses at the time of auction. Usually, farm slaves slept in different areas of the farmstead, in the shed or the outhouse. It was not uncommon for shepherds and herders to sleep outdoors in summer.

CHAPTER 10

Common Slave Culture?

Slaves captured or purchased from different countries naturally had a heterogeneous background. Christianity as a possible common religion had the potential of integrating slaves from different cultural settings, thus fostering a composite slave culture. But this did not happen in reality. Partly this had something to do with the official policy about conversion to Christianity. Seemingly, during the early years of settlement, Dutch masters were officially encouraged to convert slaves to Christianity. But for various reasons, Christianisation was far from complete.

Interaction via a common medium of communication is a precondition for the emergence of a community. According to Nigel Worden, a kind of Creole Portuguese was the lingua franca amongst slaves in the Cape. When, in 1726, Company officials interrogated the slaves of a farm, the slaves responded in many languages. One of them, Scipio of Bengal, answered in Portuguese. But Worden was careful to add that 'many newcomers did not speak it' ('Creole Portuguese') and that 'Dutch and Malay were frequently used slave languages' (Worden, 1982: 49, note 16). There are several instances of Bengali slaves who could speak only Bengali (Rugarli).

The widespread use of creolised Portuguese as a common medium of interaction, and especially as the language of commerce over several centuries, has also been reported in Cochin by Anjana Singh (2006). However, the author added that letters sent by Cochin kings to the VOC were written in Malayalam (on palm leaves), many of which are still preserved among Dutch records in the State Archives of Tamilnadu. A similar effort to locate the communications between the VOC authorities and the Mughal administrators and the local rulers of Bengal should be fruitful. That an initiative of this nature will be methodologically justified is corroborated by the fact that by the mid-seventeenth century when the Dutch established their outpost at the Cape and were operating in the Bengal delta for trade, the Mughal had established military supremacy and consolidated political power and could claim the legitimacy of their expanding political administration throughout the Gangetic delta.

A special reference is to be made here of the position of the VOC Slave Lodge. By all accounts, it remained the largest housing complex of slaves, containing around 1,000 of them in 1770 (Shell, 1997: xxxi) and constituted a quasi-autonomous slave community. Certain signs of an embryonic slave culture were to be found among slaves in the Lodge in the first half of the eighteenth century. These were manifest through recreational activities and religious (Islamic) meetings. Unfortunately, there is no way to say with certainty how many slave residents in the Slave Lodge were of Bengali origin and whether or not they formed the rudiments of a community. Later, things changed substantially when, courtesy to shifting recruitment areas, the Slave Lodge could at best assemble 'a potpourri of subcultures' (Shell, 1997: 49).

Outside the Slave Lodge, slaves were too dispersed to form a community and generate a common culture of their own. Besides, many female slaves were so closely integrated with the masters' families that they gradually became bearers of the nascent composite culture of the Cape with a marked white bias. The gender divide served additionally to weaken the possibility of ethnic slave solidarity, even where slaves in a household or a cluster of households were from the same country and spoke the same language.

All this should lead us to the conclusion that slavery in the Cape had little scope for giving rise to distinctive social and cultural forms within the slave population that characterised Afro-American communities in the Western hemisphere. The reassertive movement in the USA as a whole with reference to a specific period is sometimes referred to as the Harlem Renaissance that produced a rich flowering in the field of music and dance, a common mode of speech (African-American English or AAE), the Black Church comprising separatist and syncretistic Christian sects of the African-Americans, and the militant liberation struggles. In the Cape, residues of slave cultures have retained a weak presence in certain culinary traits, religious practices, and several isolated words and phrases which can, in general, be traced back to the Malay community.

CHAPTER 11

Protest, Resistance, and Revolt

There is no reason to suppose that Bengali slaves, as also those of other ethnicities, accepted their condition without demur. Resistance to subordination in general to which they were subjected assumed different forms such as absenteeism, dereliction of duty and delinquency of a more serious nature, desertion at both individual and collective level, arson, attempted suicide, defiance of the master's authority, and rebellion. About the last category it should be remembered that there is no recorded case of rebellion during the VOC rule that aimed at bringing down the system of slavery. It was only in 1808, after the British take-over, that an uprising (the Koeberg slave uprising of 1808) took place, seeking to overthrow the system. Two other rebellions followed (the Swartland and the Koue Bokkeveld). These have been presented below in greater detail.

Archives provide ample examples of protests of various kinds. Wilful delay in providing service was probably the most common. But it could be occasioned by genuine reasons. There have been cases in which slaves who returned home late after an errand were punished by their masters who feared that they had escaped or had tried to escape. We have the case of Fortuijn van Bengal who was charged for returning later than expected from a mission. Fortuijn's defence was that the late return happened because he had to walk a long distance to get back to his master's farmstead. Not satisfied with this plea, the enraged master hit Fortuijn and threw him to the ground. Fortuijn then took out a knife; but before he could do any harm to the master, he was overpowered by others (Worden, 1982: 51).

Desertion too was a common phenomenon. This process gained strength over the years. Aggrieved individual slaves just quit their jobs and fled from their masters' houses or farms. Escape from slave farms or households in rural areas was not difficult, given the isolated position of the Cape, the small size of a master's family, and the geography of the surrounding terrain interspersed with mountain ranges and forests that provided ideal hiding places. Table Mountain, lying not far from the fort, was a favourite hiding place for escapees throughout the eighteenth century. Later with the expansion of the Cape settlement and increase in the size of slave population, Hangklip (Hanglip according to some), on the southernmost point of False Bay, emerged as a preferred sanctuary of runaway slaves. The colony remained in existence well until the nineteenth century. Many of the criminal cases involved deserters who had taken refuge in the community of slaves at Hangklip.

An ingenious method of escape devised by some slaves was to escape to Europe by boats from the Table Bay. Some of them enrolled in VOC as sailors with the hope that they would be sent to the East where they might emerge as free men. It is not clear how many slaves made use of this device successfully; but we have found records of two slaves of the Cape (Jan van de Caab's case of 1751 and Jacob van de Caab's case of 1752) who tried this innovative method unsuccessfully and were apprehended when their ships passed through Cape Town (Worden and Groenewald, 2005: 285-88 and 302-05).

Fugitive slaves, either living in a community (e.g. Hangklip) or roving around in small groups and even individually, posed a major threat to the security of white farmers, including slave owners. This phenomenon additionally cast its shadow on slaves on farms, enticing them to join the fugitives or at least to help them with provisions and information about white farmers. An appropriate example is provided by a 1726 case in which Aaron van Bengalen was involved as a ringleader. Aaron, a cattle herd, reportedly escaped from his owner along with some other slaves and took shelter in the Blaauberg, Tygerberg, and Koeberg areas. From here, the fugitives raided nearby farmhouses and cattle posts for several months. The threat posed by them was so serious that large commando of ninety men was dispatched to contain their operations. Although, after a successful operation, nineteen slaves were charged with criminal activities, Aaron of Bengal appears to have escaped capture.

An ordinary escape not leading to violence was punished by the master himself, often brutally. Regular patrols by commandos of the administration and by search parties of individual slave owners, either single-handed or collectively, were mounted to recapture runaway slaves. 'Exemplary' punishment was reserved for recaptured slaves. Reprimanding the escapee was perhaps the mildest form of punishment; the more severe were physical assaults on the fugitive, including flogging him with a *sjambok*.

Escape and resistance offered, on being recaptured, were treated as criminal offences. The more serious cases were sent to the *landdrost* (local magistrate) and frequently to the Court of Justice in Cape Town. Even a casual look at the records reveals that an overwhelming majority of the criminal cases in the Cape dealt with escaped slaves or *drosters*, as they were called locally. Some of them were Bengalis.

Suicides were considered as escapes of a special kind – as flights to 'the point of no return'. It has been argued by some (Ward, 2006: 9) that in the slave society of the Cape ruled under the Roman-Dutch law, slave suicides were 'both a form of resistance and a crime against property'. After all, a slave was considered a piece of property belonging to the master. To cause his death (whoever might have been responsible) was to deprive the master of his belonging; the perpetrator was therefore punishable. No punishment could be inflicted, by definition, on a successful suicide. But the castle authorities saw to it that an act of this nature met with rigorous retribution. The corpse was often dragged along the main thoroughfare of the town to the gallows and was hung in public display. In doing this, the Company asserted its unchallenged entitlement to inflict its will on the corpse.

Slaves, often in desperation, avenged their maltreatment by setting fire to their master's farms. Thatched roofs of Cape farmsteads were particularly vulnerable targets. In 1717, Aaron van Bengal set fire to the roof of the wine-making building where he worked. He paid a heavy price for this act of defiance: he was burnt to death, after being tied to a pole and 'half-strangled'.

Because they were dispersed from the very beginning of their stay in the Cape, Bengali slaves do not seem to have offered an organised resistance against the system collectively. All the same, there is evidence that in individual cases of protest, they worked in tandem with slaves from other backgrounds.

It is difficult to estimate the full incidence of this phenomenon. However, we have records of individual cases. Nigel Worden (1982: 48) refers to a murder in 1791, when a *knecht* (a supervisor of slaves) flogged to death an unfortunate slave, January of Mozambique. In the murder trial that followed, Maart van Bengal, himself a slave working on the same farm, joined three other slaves from Madagascar, and one each from Mozambique and the Cape, to give evidence against the *knecht*.

Then there was the case of Manuel of Bengal. This slave based at the Cape and already past his productive years had the misfortune of being denied his freedom, although it was promised to him. Manuel had the courage to refuse to be a slave any longer and made his master's life unpleasant. He had to pay a heavy price for it as he was locked up (Shell, 1997: 400). Another episode involved Aaron van Bengal who led a group of slaves in 1726 to attack their master's *knecht*, Adam van Claaten (according to some 'Adam van Dijk'), reputedly vicious and vindictive to his subordinates (Shell, 1997: 24).

Perhaps more significant was an escape staged by several slaves in 1738. Taking advantage of the absence of their widowed mistress, the soon-to-be fugitives helped themselves with food, drink, and some clothing. Then they set off for Klipheuvel for shelter. The misadventure that ended disastrously was led by a thirty-year-old Bengali slave, Jourdaan van Bengal, who was elected 'captain' of the group and carried the only gun the group possessed.

Once in a while deserters headed, collectively, for a specific region, more often than not for a territory beyond the reach of the VOC. For example, an abortive attempt was made in 1714 by eleven runaway slaves who planned to escape to Namaqualand to the north of the Cape and beyond the reach of the VOC administration. Thomas van Bengalen, a middle-level leader of the group, was described in the official documentation as 'one of the principal inducers, inciters, and seducers of the slaves'. Thomas was caught and hanged.

Another attempt was made in 1746 when eight slaves headed for 'the land of the Caffers', i.e. the Eastern Cape; but as far as we know, no Bengali slave was involved in this unsuccessful adventure (1746 case against Januarij van Boegies et al.).

There were more organised protests. One such case was the Koeberg slave uprising of 1808, led by Louis of Mauritius, which was crushed. A second slave uprising started in Swartland (present-day Malmesbury) and was suppressed after the marching rebels reached the Salt River. Yet a third revolt took place in 1825 led by Galant van der Kaab in Koue Bokkeveld (now Cedarberg, near Ceres), as depicted in a novel by André Brink (1982). Like the other revolts, this too was put down. We can guess that some Bengali slaves joined hands with slaves of other ethnic groups in such revolts as individuals. But detailed reports are few and far between.

A form of protest, more significant than desertion, was the defiant assertion of one's psychological autonomy, even when not challenging the rationale of the system directly. Some historians such as Genovese would have us believe that this type of resistance is more revolutionary in its impact than desertion. It is significant that protests of this nature were more evident in the early and late nineteenth century (Worden and Groenewald, 2005: 612, footnote 1). Maybe, this has something to do with the success of the American War of Independence, the Haitian slave uprising, and the French Revolution, the news of which must have percolated to the Cape thanks to the stream of ships plying between Europe and the Cape.

Archives provide us with some examples. For instance, in 1793 there was the case of Caesar van Madagascar in which the accused, Caesar, asserted his 'right to speak' (*'ik moet mijn recht van spreken hebben'*, roughly translated as 'I must have my right to speak'), and when his master lashed him with a *sjambok* for this insolence, he cut it with a knife. This 'crime' was sufficient to earn Caesar a sentence of twenty-five years of hard labour in chains on Robben Island. There were several other instances of slaves verbally articulating their defiance to the masters.

Yet with all these protests, the Cape witnessed no slave revolts in general as it happened in the New World. Historians have attempted to account for this phenomenon variously. First, it was noted that the tiny size of slave-owning families, in contrast with the size of the plantations in other countries, resulted in a relatively small number of slaves in the Cape and thus militated against slave protests assuming massive proportions. It is true that slaves generally outnumbered the masters, but the slave-master ratio was never sufficiently tilted in favour of slaves.

Further, despite creolisation (i.e. the process of slaves being born in the Cape), slaves who were natives of other territories decisively outnumbered the Creole slaves born locally. The backgrounds of these foreign-born slaves were varied in terms of ethnicity, language, and religion. In the absence of a composite cultural identity, there was little likelihood of a general slave revolt mobilising such disparate elements in a massive thrust against the system. Finally, the social structure of the slave-holding regime did not permit the emergence of an autonomous black leadership.

VOC authorities followed a two-pronged policy to deal with such threats. There were strong measures to suppress slave resistance, actual or threatened, combined with steps to enhance slaves' dependence on the owners. For the latter purpose, dependence on drugs (such as *arrack* or rice wine, tobacco, and marijuana) was encouraged. Additionally, stringent laws and ordinances posed a negative sanction against occurrence of violence among slaves. Rigorous punishment, often corporal in nature, was the commonest form of control. The instruments used included flogging the 'guilty' person with *sjambok*, putting him or her in fetters, confinement, sometimes for a period exceeding several years at a stretch, 'live impaling' for arsonists and making him or her work without pay. In the colourful languages of Robert Ross, 'It is as if the machine of production required to be oiled by the blood flogged out of the slaves' backs' (quoted by Shell, 1997: 206).

In their recently published book, *Trials of Slavery*, Nigel Worden and Gerald Groenewald have provided verbatim records of trials involving Cape slaves during the eighteenth century. Some of these relate to Bengali slaves. In one such episode, the experiences of two Bengali slaves, Dela and Flora, are narrated *(CJ 387 Criminele Process Stukken*, 1766, ff. 132-34). In this, Dela, the deponent, made a formal complaint in 1766 against Godfried Heijns for mercilessly thrashing Flora, his slave.

Yet, in law, slaves were protected from being badly beaten. The authorities allowed owners the right to inflict only 'mild domestic chastisement'[9] on slaves. This was defined as the type of punishment that could be meted out justifiably to one's wife and children. Anglophiles may note with justifiable pride that the British administration abolished physical torture after the occupation of the Cape, but then, ironically, the scope of 'domestic punishment' still allowed 25 lashes! The authorities additionally allowed slaves to take their grievances to the Fiscal, a top official under the Dutch administration, and to the protector of slaves, a post created by the British administration after 1817.

Another weapon in the hands of masters was 'punishment sales' (e.g. Shell: 96-97). A relatively severe crime was followed by the banishment of the person responsible for the crime to the Cape's penal colony, Robben Island. Besides, the death sentence was frequently pronounced, sometimes for offences that would not in a modern society be considered so serious as to call for capital punishment. Robert Shell says, between 1680 and 1795, 'almost one slave per month was publicly executed in Cape Town' (1997: 193). The total number of executed slaves, in this period, comes to more than 1,200. In most cases, the execution was preceded by torture and followed by the dragging of the body through the streets of the town.

In fairness, we should add that dispensation of punishment of this nature was in theory the prerogative of Company officials. But more often than not, this was violated by private slave owners. There are records to show that the latter were reprimanded in some cases. Diana van Bengalen provides a suitable instance. Her master, the burgher Daniel (Michiel) Lorich, wishing to punish her for 'an act of misdemeanour', ordered another of his slaves to whip Diana. Diana died as a result. Two surgeons from the VOC hospital were assigned the task of determining the cause of Diana's death but were reportedly unable to establish the grounds of Diana's death. However, the behaviour of Lorich was considered a threat to the settlement. He was, therefore, banished from the Cape and sent back to the Netherlands. In mitigation, supporters of the system may argue that physical punishment was not limited to slaves but was extended additionally to Khoi workers and even to European indentured labourers, sailors, and soldiers.

The VOC administration took some supplementary measures to prevent trouble at night. There were curfew laws that directed owners to ensure that slaves were restricted to the house after nightfall. Slaves sent out on nocturnal missions were required to carry their letter of authorisation to go out beyond curfew hours—a practice that was followed with greater thoroughness during the apartheid regime in a different context and with regard to all black Africans.

CHAPTER 12

Incorporation of Bengali Slaves into Mainstream Cape Society

As mentioned earlier, descendants of Bengali slaves are now fully absorbed into the mainstream Cape Town society. Currently, this consists of five ethnic groups: (a) the whites divided between the English-speaking and the Afrikaans-speaking people (Afrikaners), (b) the Coloured group or the people of mixed Afro-European blood who generally speak Afrikaans as their first language, (c) descendants of the Khoisan communities who now speak Afrikaans as their first language and who are regarded as forming a part of the Coloured group, (d) Cape Malays, Afrikaans speakers and mainly Muslim by religion, and (e) black Africans who are generally Xhosa speakers, many of them having migrated from Eastern Cape. The generic term 'Coloured' consists broadly of the categories (b), (c), and (d).

The present-day white population is a composite product of diverse elements that came to the Cape from the Netherlands, Britain, and Germany, several Scandinavian countries such as Sweden and Denmark, and France at different times. Currently, this group is divided broadly between those who speak English as their first language and those whose first language is Afrikaans. French Protestant refugees, Huguenots, who began coming to the Cape starting from the close of the seventeenth century, are now fully assimilated into the group whose first language is Afrikaans. Ethnic differences apart, whites traditionally demonstrated considerable occupational differences. There were soldiers, sailors, traders, including slave traders, farmers, herders, and artisans whose ranks were joined later by those who came in search of a quick fortune—the adventurers.

The Cape Malays still retain their distinctive characteristics. Unlike other constituents of the Coloured group, they follow Islamic tenets. Many of them trace their origin from the East, the Indonesian archipelago to be more precise, to which were grafted some individuals and families from India who professed Islam. The Malays are also distinguished by their residential separation. In Cape Town, they were previously settled in such near-exclusive neighbourhoods as Bo-Kaap and District Six.

Some of the free blacks and several Bengali slave owners were gradually assimilated into the Christian white mainstream of Cape society. Yet, Robert Shell may be right in saying that the success of the few manumitted slave women in crossing the racial line in this period may not be regarded as 'real evidence of racial fluidity' (1994/97: 324). However, the conditions under which such assimilation took place merit some discussion. Antonia Malan made a distinction between male and female free blacks. 'Those women who retained the family property in their own hands as widows could control its redistribution to their children and sons-in-law. A woman who married a European immigrant and produced sons and daughters could see her grandchildren prosper as colonists' (Malan, 1998-99: 66-67).

To conclude, the process of assimilation varied from case to case and from period to period. For able-bodied women who were employed as domestic helps and especially as wet nurses in white households, the process of incorporation was less difficult. A number of them gained acceptance into the white community through marriage. It is true that Jan Pietersz Coen, governor general of Batavia for several years in the early seventeenth century, made a strong plea for the dispatch of young Dutch women to settlements in Africa and Asia so that an autonomous Burgher community could come into being there, but this met with little success. Absence of suitable female partners led to the practice of concubinage; but this was banned in 1620. Thus, intermarriage with local women, especially Asian and Eurasian, was not looked down upon.

Some slaves of both sexes were fortunate enough to be freed by their masters, but their number was not too large. A few are known to have purchased their own freedom. The rest were manumitted on a variety of grounds, e.g. faithful and caring service, acceptance of the major traits of the dominant group such as the prevailing tenets of the Dutch Reformed Church, and knowledge of the Dutch language. For Bengali male slaves, successful completion of this process was extremely rare.

Formal incorporation into the dominant, Christian, stream of Cape society facilitated the assimilation process. However, integration with the multi-ethnic

Cape society took place at other levels too. A number of Bengali slaves found their way to the growing Islamic community of the Malay-dominated Cape Coloured people, especially in the late eighteenth and early nineteenth centuries. There were others who too were absorbed into the Cape Coloured people but remained Christian. Finally, an indeterminate number of Bengali slaves lost their separate identity in the vast composite black group.

Seemingly, the process of incorporation became harder with the passage of time when racial attitudes of the white settlers became less tolerant. This may have something to do with the increase in the size of non-white population, and the growing confidence of burghers in the future of their settlement.

A step in the assimilation process was the manumission of the slave and his or her economic and social rehabilitation. Slaves achieved freedom under different circumstances and on different basis. Rules governing manumission of slaves of the Slave Lodge that governed the relevant transactions for more than a century (1685-1795) owed much to Adriaan van Reede tot Drakenstein, the visiting commissioner. A summary of the regulations made under his auspices should be relevant to our discussion.

The van Reede proposal has been hailed as 'a milestone' in slave administration in the Cape (Schoeman, 2007: 327) for the thoroughness with which it dealt with the issue. Its basic conclusion was that imported male and female slaves should be freed after thirty years of service, but it should be noted at the same time that manumission was a favour and not a right. There were several conditions attached to the provision of manumission.

1.   *Slaves going to be manumitted must have served their owners conscientiously and faithfully.*
2.   *They should be able to speak Dutch reasonably well.*
3.   *They must have been 'confirmed' in the Church.*
4.   *They had to prove their capacity of earning their living to the authorities.*
5.   *The slave about to be manumitted would be required to pay 100 Florins as the price of his or her freedom.*
6.   *When these conditions have been met, the Political Council would pass a specific resolution authorising the manumission.*

Not surprisingly, only three slaves during the entire period obtained their freedom in terms of these provisions. We may like to note that one of them was from Bengal. Those who would go by statistics would find that only 0.0005 per cent of imported slaves could achieve this glorious finale (Shell, 1997: 375).

For those who could not pay the price, there was a provision for a substitute slave. In 1764, Anna, daughter of Jacoba of the Cape, applied for emancipation and offered Cupido of Bengal, a twelve-year-old boy, as a substitute slave. A surgeon's certificate attached to the petition confirmed that the boy was healthy and strong.

There were other regulations that dealt with manumission of privately owned slaves (Shell, 1997: 377). After 1708, an owner planning to manumit a slave had to give an undertaking that the freed slave would not be an encumbrance on the administration for ten years. In 1722, in addition to the undertaking, an application for manumission had to be accompanied by letters of support from two guarantors who were generally relatives of the owner.

Hattingh (1981: 37) gives a list of the cases between 1701 and 1720 that led to slaves being freed in the Cape. The list is at best illustrative. But it does point to the trend. It shows that during the first two decades of the eighteenth century, a total of 143 slaves were freed. In some cases, the action was backed by several justifications, which is why the reasons given outnumbered the freed slaves in the list. Of the 238 reasons recorded, baptism accounted for only 11, while knowledge of the Dutch language led to freedom in 28 cases. The most frequently cited reason (57) was faithful service rendered to the owner. Angela van Bengalen's manumission in 1666 was perhaps one of the earliest cases of this kind. When her master, Hendrik Gabbema, was asked about the reason of his magnanimity, he is quoted as saying 'uit pure genegenheid'—'simply out of affection'.

In a few cases, Burgher slave owners extended their bounty beyond manumission. In 1688, Hans Rutgertroost appointed Maria van Bengale and the two children he fathered 'his universal heirs' (Schoeman, 2007: 257). In 1726, a burgher in Stellenbosch gifted his entire estate to his slave, Carel van Bengal (Shell, 1997: 223).

Hattingh made a rough calculation of the outcome of the process with regard to certain marriages or relationships involving whites and non-whites. According to him, currently the total number of Lijsbeth van Bengale's descendants can be between 243,000 and 246,000 (cited by Heese, 1984: 12). However, these took place in the early decades of Dutch rule in the Cape. Given the pervasive racial bias that emerged later among large sections of the white population, this genealogical feature remained a taboo, not to be mentioned or even hinted at in polite conversation among whites. In 1984, Hans Heese, himself an Afrikaner, argued in a well documented book, *Groep sonder Grense* (*Community without*

Boundaries), that more than one thousand Afrikaner families are descendants of slaves in the early period of VOC rule. The families concerned were so outraged that they took the matter to court for defamation in a million-rand suit.

Things changed later. Today quite a few South Africans, including a considerable number of Afrikaners, are no longer ashamed of their non-white ancestry. Currently, the Internet carries several websites put up by some of them to demonstrate, by means of genealogical trees, how specifically they are descended from a slave ancestor or ancestress (e.g. A.M. van Rensburg, *My Genetic Enrichment: Slaves at the Cape, South Africa*, website: <Tandre@ rensburg.com>).

Several interesting stories relating to the issue are now doing the rounds. One of them centres on the exploits of Catharina of Palicatte or Groote Catrijn Snyman as she was generally known. Catharina was condemned to death in Batavia for causing murder to her consort, but her sentence was commuted afterwards. She was then banished to the Cape as a bandiet (convict) in early 1657. There she was romantically involved with a white soldier, Hans Christoffel Snijder (or Snijman), from Heidelberg. Their illegitimate son Christoffel Snijman was baptised on 9 March 1669, and the manumitted slave Angela van Bengalen was one of his godparents. Thanks to her liaisons with an assortment of well-off whites and free blacks, Groote Catrijn's status had been enhanced to a considerable extent by the early 1670s, and she obtained a free pardon for her crime and a permission to marry into the bargain. In December 1671, she chose as her husband a moderately prosperous free black, Anthonij Jansz of Bengal. The couple was childless, but Anthonij was stepfather to at least two of his wife's mixed-race children, Petronella and Christoffel. When both Anthonij and Groote Catrijn died within a short interval, Christoffel Snijman's godmother, Angela of Bengal, presumably took charge of the young man.

Christoffel later acquired a farm at Groot Drakenstein where he lived with his bride, Marguerite Thérèse de Savoye, whose father was a well-known French Huguenot. In the following several centuries, the Snymans of Groote Catrijn's clan contracted matrimonial relations with many Afrikaner families. The first prime minister of the Union of South Africa, General Louis Botha, was a descendant of Groote Catrijn's granddaughter, Marie Snyman, whose husband was Theunis Botha (Jackie Loos, 'Catharina of Palicatte' in Shell (Ed.) *Diaspora to Diorama*, p. 387).

An equally dramatic admission of a link of this nature has come from former president of South Africa Frederik Willem de Klerk, an important architect of the apartheid regime, who now acknowledges a Bengali slave ancestry (Margot Hornblower, 'Roots Mania' in *Time in Partnership with CNN*, Monday, July 30, 2007). Perhaps the boldest and the most striking assertion of this heritage has come from Professor Robert Shell: 'The truth is, we are all the descendants of slavery' (1994: xix).

During my visit to South Africa in 2003-04, I had the good fortune of meeting Therese Benadé, an Afrikaner lady, who claimed that she was the thirteenth descendant of Angela van Bengalen. She added she was proud of her pedigree and would like to publicise it through a book she was in the process of writing. The book originally written in English, *Kites of Good Fortune*, was subsequently published by David Philip in 2004. An Afrikaans translation, *Anna, Dogter van Angela van Bengale*, came out in 2005. The genealogical chart drawn for the present author by Therese Benadé is reproduced here as Appendix E.

The process of going back to the roots was fostered by a considerable amount of interest created by various genealogical societies of South Africa. The South African Genealogical Society through its journal, *Familia*, has been reconstructing genealogical trees of whites of the Cape. An important publication in this field is the *Suid-Afrikaanse Geslagsregisters* or *South African Genealogies*. For other genealogical details, old files of the *Kronos* (*Journal of Cape History*) and *Capensis* are of considerable help.

Additionally, energetic support has been extended to this development by various historical societies that have been encouraging community research and individual attempts at discovering the past. Some Cape Malays have even been going to Indonesia in search of their roots.

Understandably, genealogical reconstruction of persons with European origin proved to be comparatively easier than that of descendants of slaves married to non-Europeans. This has been shown convincingly by Antonia Malan of the University of Cape Town while tracing the line of descent of Henrietta Claasz Wittebol, daughter of Klaas Gerrits of Bengal. Henrietta married Johann Claus Möller or Mülder of Hamburg; which made it possible for her five descendants to acquire genealogically traceable status (1998-99: 55). By contrast, her brothers' children vanished 'into the genealogical shadows' because they did not continue with the family name.

CHAPTER 13

Malays[10] vs. Indians as the Core Coloured Group

Cape society to which slaves from Bengal were brought witnessed the emergence of a Coloured community in the seventeenth and eighteenth centuries. It is well known that while descendants of Euro-African mixed marriages constituted its hard core, forced migrants of the Malay-Indonesian archipelago also contributed to its formation and growth. A specific thrust of this book is the thesis that from mid-eighteenth century onwards some freed Bengali slaves (and free blacks) were being drawn to Islam and gradually incorporated into the Coloured community. We do not know how numerous such people were. But given the limited number of freed Bengali slaves being accepted in the white community, the size of the Muslim Bengali community may not have been insignificant.

Islam was introduced in the Cape by political exiles from the East Indies. Such important political deportees included, among other persons, Radja (King) of Tamborah who is often mentioned in contemporary documents.[11]

Time and again, it is said that the Dutch authorities hardly made any effort to convert slaves to Christianity mainly because of the VOC rule that, once baptised, a slave could not be sold. Conversion to Christianity, therefore, devalued the potential market of the slave. However, we have to take this view with some reservation.

The official policy regarding manumission, and especially the conditions attached to it, varied from one dependency to another and within the same dependency, from one period to another (Shell, 1997: 359-60). Further, the manner in which the policy was enforced often went against its avowed thrust.

A glaring instance of this disconnection is the case of Clasina of Bengal. As far as is known, Clasina had the distinction of being the one and only slave in the whole history of Cape slavery to claim her free woman status on the grounds that she was actually never sold into slavery and had, in fact, been baptised as a Christian. The request was made in terms of the recommendations of the Synod of Dordrecht in the Netherlands (Dord, in short) of 1618-19 which said, inter alia, that baptised slaves should be allowed to enjoy the same freedom as other Christians.[12] But Clasina's complaint was rejected in 1809. The legal technicalities of this case, detailed by Shell (1997: 365), might have intrigued lawyers but did not, sadly, offer any help to slaves seeking freedom on this account.

Islam, on the other hand, provided a social link to free blacks and the aristocratic exiles from Indonesia. Officers of the VOC noted the growth of a positive feeling towards Islam among the slaves in the Cape. Islam spread during the second half of the eighteenth and the first half of the nineteenth centuries. William Bird, a government employee, wrote about this in the early 1820s. Commenting on the small number of baptisms in this period, he said, with marked sarcasm, that Christian education was almost non-existent. And where it was provided for, it comprised only two of the Ten Commandments, telling the converted not to steal or kill. Bird did not elaborate, but the point is obvious.

Some Bengali slaves, Muslims by religion, held high official positions in the Dutch administration. Others occupied important posts in the Islamic religious order such as the office of *imam* in well-known mosques or were otherwise community leaders. Indeed, according to Davids, Islam in the Cape was spread 'mainly by Indian Muslim slaves from Bengal' (quoted by Todescini, 2003: 5).

Frans of Bengal, originally a slave, combined both roles after manumission. In 1800, at the head of a Muslim delegation, he requested Sir George Young to grant the local Muslim community a site for a mosque in Venderleur Street in District Six of Cape Town (Achmat, 1989). Interestingly, Frans signed his name in Arabic characters in the memorandum, a trend that is suggestive of the emergence of Arabic-Afrikaans as a means of communication among the non-white underclass. Community leadership was combined by Frans with running a high office in administration, as he is known to have led the *Javaansche* (Javanese) Artillery at the battle of Blouberg in 1806. Achmat of Bengal who later became the Imam of the Dorpstreet mosque in Cape Town provides another famous illustration. Interestingly, Islamisation at this stage remained incomplete insofar as a number of Muslim Bengalis did not use typical Islamic names.

Under these circumstances, it seems odd that Malays, and not descendants of Indians, now occupy the central core of the Coloured group in the Cape. After all, the number of slaves from India could compare more than favourably with that from the Malay-Indonesian archipelago.

However, in the mid-seventeenth century and in the decades following, slaves from India were divided between Bengalis, Malayalam speakers from the Malabar Coast, and the 'Coromandelians', presumably Telugu and Tamil speakers. They were obviously without a common speech and a common religion and did not, in all likelihood, think of themselves as Indians.

Malays, in contrast, had a stronger sense of identity and solidarity than Indians. Although their first languages were different such as Ambonese, Balinese, Bouginese (or the Bugis language), Javanese, Maccasar, and Sundanese, Malays had a common speech, Malayu (or Malaya), that later formed the basis of the national language of Indonesia, Bahasa Indonesia. People from the Indonesian archipelago were additionally united by a common religion, Islam. What is more, although they were dispersed like Indian slaves, several princes and other noble men (e.g. Radja of Tamborah, Abulbasi) who were exiled in the Cape from Indonesia provided a kind of rallying point for Malays. Also religious leaders, e.g., Tuan Guru[13] (original name, Abdullah bin Kadi Abdus-Salaam) and Sheikh Yusuf of Makassar, a member of the royal house of Goa (or Gowa) in Macassar who was revered as a Muslim saint, cemented this bond. The string of mosques and tomb shrines (*keramats*) of religious leaders in the Cape peninsula institutionalised it with considerable effect. Ironically, in putting a religious coating on people like Sheikh Yusuf, their original status in Cape society was sometimes conveniently forgotten, for Yusuf was exiled to the Cape primarily as a political prisoner by the VOC, with a substantial entourage permitted to travel with him.

Cohesion among migrants from the Indonesian archipelago was vividly manifested on certain occasions such as several attempted group escapes staged by slaves from the Cape to freedom. An episode which is particularly noteworthy is the criminal case of 1751 brought against Januarij van Boegies et al. (Worden and Groenewald, 2005: 288-97). The case relates to two groups of slaves. The first group had ten runaway men who had recently arrived from South-East Asia. Apparently four of them were never apprehended.

Of the remaining six, four were killed by a commando, one escaped, and the remaining slave was captured. The escapade happened in mid-January, and the drama ended with the commando raid on the fugitive slaves around 2 February. The news of this incident soon reached Cape Town embellished with customary hyperbole. Statements like 'recently a group of slaves escaped and has already arrived safely in a free *negerij* (a community of black people) or even in Madagascar' proved sufficiently inspiring to goad other slaves to action. Thus, it is that on 13 February, a second group of twelve slaves and a 'bandiet' (convict) escaped. The attempt failed disastrously with the capture of eleven of them, while the remaining two were shot dead.

The relevance of this two-part episode to the present discussion should be clear. All actors of this drama were from the Indonesian archipelago ('*alle Oosterlingen*', i.e. 'all Orientals'), suggesting the existence of a communication and social network among migrants from this region. This was clearly strengthened by the prevalence of a common language, Malay, which the escapees employed for verbal interaction. They additionally made use of South-East Asian weapons in their fights against commandos, though not with the expected degree of success, and war cries.

Contribution of ethnicity to group solidarity was even clearer in the events surrounding the criminal case of 1760 against Achilles van de West Cust et al. This time the actors were all from the Bugis or Boegies, a part of modern Indonesia, which several documents referred to as '*de Boegies natie*' ('the Bugis nation'). The case reveals how traditional notions of Bugi medicine and conventional practices to fight diseases were effectively used by the escapees in their dangerous exploits. It shows additionally how, despite widespread illiteracy, letters written in the Bugis language could work as a cementing factor among them. Indeed, a letter used by the escapees was said to have the power to protect their bodies from evil. The strength of Bugis ethnicity was furthermore reflected in the way kinship terms such as 'father' and 'brother' were freely employed to refer to escapees of appropriate age and standing (Worden and Groenewald, 2005: 355-84).

A contrast with Bengali slaves could not be more apparent. Certainly, the number of Bengali slaves was considerable, and the common language could provide a central focus. However, as has been said above, Bengali slaves were dispersed geographically right from the beginning. More often than not, even members of the same family were sold to different purchasers. In addition, there was no indication of a continuity of slave names as slaves carried no surnames and slave children were designated differently from their parents, depending on the place of birth in each case. In consequence, a kinship network that is usually accompanied by the practice of bearing a common name, based on consanguinity, could not emerge. To be sure, this characteristic feature applied also to slaves from other regions of the subcontinent. Migrants from Indonesian archipelago, by contrast, evolved and utilised other bonds of integration. Consequently, the continuity of family and community lines was easier in their case.

The relative stability of the slave family that had characterised slave societies elsewhere such as those in North America was simply non-existent in the Cape. There was gender imbalance in the slave population, the balance being tilted in favour of males (see Tables 2, 5, and 6). Some slaves did form stable marital unions, but before the nineteenth century, no slave marriage, not solemnised by Christian rites, was admissible in law. The small size of the average farm that employed slaves could not ensure the degree of privacy needed for a family unit. Another factor inhibiting family stability was the absence of parental control over children that was severely restricted by the authority of slave owners. Where slave families did exist, they tended to be matrifocal.

Isolated and surrounded by persons of other ethnic categories, Bengali slaves and their descendants were deracinated more than their Malay counterparts and gradually lost their separate identity through a double assimilation process. A number of manumitted slaves, mainly women and their children became part of the local white society via marriage. Well-known examples include the offspring of Maria of Bengal, Angela of Bengal, Anna de Koning, and Louis of Bengal. Indeed, some observers such as Helena Liebenberg (*Introduction to Resolutions of the Council of Policy of Cape of Good Hope*) believe that of all the ethnic communities, the slaves from Bengal adapted most successfully to Cape society.

All these cases occurred during the second half of the seventeenth century and early decades of the eighteenth century. According to Shell, over a thousand women descended from slaves and 'natives' (i.e. Khoi or, to use a popular, though derogatory, term, 'Hottentottine') were married to burghers of European descent, facilitating their absorption into the European community (1994: 329). Bengali slave women must have comprised a fair proportion of unions of this nature.

It will be wrong to assume that marriage partners were randomly selected by the two parties, and particularly by the white slave owner. Clearly, female Bengali slaves had hardly any choice in the matter. After all, manumission followed by marriage with the owner was a stroke of luck for them, 'an escape mechanism from slavery' as Heese has characterised it (Heese, *Groep*: 8). But for white slave owners who had a greater freedom to choose, preference in terms of race and origin was important. Stereotypes about slaves of various 'somatic' brands were prevalent among slave owners at that time. Such stereotypes of Bengali slaves have been noted by different observers. Thus, Bengali slaves together with slaves from other parts of India and Indonesia were favoured for industrial work and services, while African slaves were chosen for farm labour. The adroit needle work of female Asian slaves has been noted earlier (see pp. 21-22).

An example of how stereotyping resulted in varying incidence of marriage by racial origin may be of interest. According to one estimate, of the 191 slave women who married or lived with white men from regions speaking German or other languages closely related to German during the seventeenth and early eighteenth centuries, more than 15 per cent were from Bengal (Shell, 1997: 322). Marriages of Maria, Angela, Anna de Koning, and Louis of Bengal all took place during this period. But the situation changed for worse later. Interracial marriage became less common. Undoubtedly, marriage between male ex-slaves and white burgher women was rare by all accounts.

In several cases, the ethnic mélange involving a series of marriages was elaborate and colourful, with striking effects. H. F. Heese mentions the case of Helena Valentyn, daughter of Hercules Valentyn of the (Coromandel) 'Kust' (Coast) and Cecilia van Bengale, who was married to the son of 'Radja' (king) of Tamborah in modern-day Indonesia. The groom was born a Muslim and carried an Islamic name, Ibrahim Adahaan. Later, on being converted to Christianity, his name was changed to Abraham de Haan. The Christian couple had five children of whom two were boys. According to the prevailing practice, the two sons apparently had no difficulty in getting accepted in white society. Even the children of the three daughters who married white men were assimilated into white society. The daughter of a Bengali slave woman (who could well have been born in a Hindu family) married a Muslim Malay prince, who later converted to Christianity. The couple had five children, all of whom were assimilated into white (and presumably, Christian) society. Could we have a more fascinating example of the ethnic brew that laid the foundation of Cape society?

In the assimilation process, a step higher than the slave status was that of *vryswarts* ('free blacks'), consisting almost entirely of liberated slaves. The free blacks were ex-slaves from different countries, including those from India, Indonesia, and China (in a few cases). According to Elphick and Giliomee

(1989, quoted by Heese, 1984: 21), Bengali free blacks formed the largest single group of the descendants of free blacks (19.5%) in 1705; the proportion of free blacks from the whole of Asia was 61 per cent in the same year.

There is some controversy regarding the position of free blacks in early Cape society. Leon Hattingh asserted that Stellenbosch was still an 'open society' in the early eighteenth century with manumission, mixed marriages, and miscegenation considerably in vogue. The social network binding Gerrit Coetsé Jacobsz, a burgher accused of sodomy, with several free blacks implicated in the trial, bears testimony to this (Newton-King, 2006). This assessment was opposed by Elphick, Shell, and Giliomee, who argued that racial prejudice and discrimination had already become part of the overall social structure of the Cape and that there was a high degree of correlation between race and class and little upward mobility for non-whites. Recently, Karel Schoeman has lent support to this view by analysing the court cases of Daniel Rodrigo (1698), Flora van Bengalen (1718-19), and Pieter Brasman or Pieter van de Caab (1708) and drawing our attention to the racial and social class undertones behind the judgments meted out to them (2007).

It is likely that the position of free blacks was already turning for the worse with the onset of the eighteenth century. In 1722, for instance, Cape Town saw the formation of a separate militia for free blacks. Under this new dispensation, free blacks were forbidden to carry arms, with the specific instruction that they would be expected to fight incidents of fire and to put a stop to the plundering of shipwrecks. The requirement that members of free black militia would serve under the command of officers from their own group gave further credence to the belief that the measure was aimed at impeding their upward social mobility.

Finally, may I pose a brainteaser to the enterprising anthropologist? How would you explain the emergence and functioning of a matrilineal formation in a society that was patently patrilineal? In the Cape during the seventeenth and nineteenth centuries, the legal lines of descent for both slaves and freed slaves were matrilineal, while the rest of the society remained firmly rooted in 'patrilineality', if we may use this term. In other words, whether one was slave or free depended upon the status of one's mother, not the father. The male did not come into account. Clearly, this position was in general accord with the matter-of-factness of motherhood, while in highlighting the possibility of any controversy surrounding paternity, popular biology gains over the extant kinship ideology.

CHAPTER 14

Conclusion

Slave studies have attained a measure of academic respectability on the international scene. Several serious investigations about the institution of slavery, including slave trade, have come out during the past half-century. Some of these centre on the controversy as to whether there was a slave mode of production (or a slave-owning mode of production, according to some). In India, hardly any attempt has been made so far to join the theoretical debate on the nature of slavery. In fact, we cannot even speak of a systematic discourse on the role of slavery in Indian society, although some work has been done on the institution in ancient India, e.g. S. A. Dange's *India: From Primitive Communism to Slavery* and Dev Raj Chanana's *Slavery in Ancient India*, a doctoral thesis submitted to Sorbonne and later published as a book.

The focus of this section is limited. It concentrates on the position of Bengali slaves in Cape society from the middle of the seventeenth century to the mid-1850s. There are many references to Bengali slaves in South African and Dutch documents during this period, but unfortunately, very little is known in India about this chapter of Bengal's 'diaspora' involving South Africa.

This is despite the fact that some attempts are currently being made to study Indian diaspora (cf. Jayaram, 2004) under the auspices of the Indian Council for Social Science Research, the Indian Sociological Society, the Global Organization of People of Indian Origin, and the India International Centre. In 1995, the University Grants Commission set up a centre for the study of Indian diaspora at the University of Hyderabad, putting an official stamp of approval on the academic relevance of the subject. Unfortunately, forced migration from India to the Cape has so far remained a closed chapter to Indian social scientists and others interested in socio-historical research on India, with special reference to Indo-African relations.

Elsewhere, the response of various Indian migrant communities to new environments, leading to their adaptation to and possible integration with the host society, has been studied by social scientists. This has been attempted with reference to South-East Asia, East and South Africa, the West Indies, the UK, and the USA, among other regions. Hugh Tinker has, for instance, sought to classify Indian outward movement during the colonial era into migration by (a) indentured labour, (b) *kangani* (foremen and overseers) and *maistry* (supervisors) labour, and (c) 'passage' or 'free' labour. But such a categorisation is not especially pertinent to the present study. This is understandable because Tinker's analysis was, after all, limited to the period between 1830 and 1920, while the slave trade was banned in British territories (including the Cape) as early as 1807. What is more, Tinker was considering the cases of Indian migrants, not as individuals but as organised communities, however loosely they were structured.

Nor was the concept of 'sandwich culture' to connote 'a new pattern of interrelationship between different elements' particularly helpful in such an analysis. Yogesh Atal (quoted by Jayaram, 2004) applied a model using this concept in his effort to interpret the response of Indian migrant communities to their respective host societies. This may be useful for the study of migrants who retained their identity as a group. We should not forget that, right from the beginning, Bengali slaves were dispersed and interacted only *as individuals* with different host communities at various levels of Cape society.

More importantly, can the mere use of the term 'sandwich' explain either the process of intercultural interchange or its end product? Do we know who initiated the process and who set out its parameters? Understandably, a sandwich is a mixture of diverse elements. The question is, how should we identify the disparate components of a 'sandwich', weigh their impact on the host as well as the guest society, and throw light on the manner in which they stick together, with what consequences?

Clearly, the development of heuristic tools can be undertaken only in relation to concrete empirical issues. Indian forced migration to the Cape has remained an uncharted domain, and any attempt to apply to the subject a conceptual schema that has been developed elsewhere may not be useful. By all accounts, this amnesia at the macro level is unfortunate. The tragedy is heightened when we realise that, at the grass root level, we will probably never be able to reconstruct the world that Bengali slaves made for themselves and for Cape society. Similarly, we can in no way recreate the tales of the injustice, oppression and consequent frustration they faced, bare physical survival of many of them minus a social identity, loss of their cultural distinctiveness, painful adjustment they made to the plural society of the Cape, and their ultimate incorporation and assimilation into different communities—white, Coloured, and black.

The process of assimilation was undoubtedly tortuous for most slaves and depended on the specific circumstances in which they found themselves. It is possible that there was a rough pattern in all this. But who would venture a generalisation and interpretation of the process, even if its broad contours could be identified? The profile of the interaction between two cultures and societies, as different from each other as Calvinist Europe and medieval Bengal, might have had an overriding presence everywhere. But how much of it was diluted in concrete circumstances and with what effect is far from clear. And, above all, where we should factor the individual's role in this negotiation process can at best be guessed.

The several concepts advanced by social scientists to capture the course of assimilation elsewhere, such as 'resilience' and 'sandwich culture' (Atal in Jayaram, 2004: 208-16), are not found to be relevant to the present case, as Bengali slaves never constituted a community with a distinctive collective identity. If there was any resilience of Bengali slaves in the interaction with members of other communities in the Cape, it was at best resilience at the individual level. And the less-than organic 'sandwiching' of two distinct ways of life practiced by isolated individuals cannot be said to constitute a culture per se because culture, if anything, is always shared by members of a group. In whatever ways an individual Bengali slave adjusted himself or herself to the new context had little *immediate and direct* impact on his or her master or mistress and on fellow Bengali slaves living elsewhere in Cape society.

To be sure, the comment made above is valid for all slaves. But it is especially relevant to Bengali, Malabari, and Coromandelian slaves from India and slaves from what today is Indonesia. This is because these peoples even at that time had a more articulated, though limited, cultural heritage, including a literary tradition. As far as Bengal is concerned, we should not forget that the slave raiding and trading we are discussing in this treatise was taking place in Bengal roughly two hundred years after Chandidas (Boru) had composed *SriKrishna-kirtan*. About the same time saw the composition of the Bengali *Ramayana* by Krittivas that had attained immense popularity among Hindu

Bengalis. About half a century earlier, Mukundaram composed *Kavikankana Chandi*, another landmark in Bengal's literary tradition. It is true that many Bengali slaves could not read or write. Angela of Bengal is known to have been one of them. According to Therese Armstrong (2008) (*Rags to Riches*), Angela signed two important documents, concerning her affairs directly, with an X. One of them granted her a small plot of land on her manumission. The second one was an inventory prepared by her following the death of her husband. We also get references to the pathetically low level of literacy even where it existed. But it is well to remember that this did not prevent some of the 'literate' persons from signing documents in exotic caricature. Louis van Bengalen confessed that he did not know how to read. Yet he used a kind of 'signature' consistently. To quote Hattingh's colourful description of this: 'The signature took the form of a vertical line for the L, while the V and B were linked together in the shape of a fan' (Shoeman quoting Hattingh: 312).

There is, thus, no reason to suppose that all Bengali slaves were illiterate. Yet, we do not have anything that Bengali slaves might have told others regarding how they felt surviving as slaves, powerless, and often voiceless, in a strange and distant land, isolated almost totally from people with whom they could have meaningfully shared their thoughts, feelings, sufferings, and memories of homeland through a common medium.

The contrast with the historiography of antebellum USA clearly comes to mind. Eugene Genovese (1976) reconstructed 'the world (African-American) slaves made', using a variety of sources. He meticulously explored an immense volume of official documents and supplemented his data with information collected from interviews with ex-slaves carried out by various researchers. A great boon to students and researchers was the publication of the transcripts of the interviews by Greenwood Press in Westport, Connecticut. According to Genovese, as many as thirty-five volumes of such accounts have been brought out. In addition, he consulted more than 200 relevant manuscript collections kept at the University of North Carolina and Louisiana State University. Despite all this, Genovese grimly concludes 'that all the sources are treacherous and that no 'definitive' study has been or ever will be written' (1976: 676).

In the Cape, there are very few surviving documents of this period that were written in a language other than Dutch, English, Portuguese, and Arabic. Possibly the two letters written in Singhalese mentioned under endnote 14 of this monograph lie somewhere in the archives, indecipherable and unread. There is also the oft-quoted letter written in the Buginese or Bouginese language using its distinctive script.[14] Although Buginese is spoken in a small coastal area in the Celebes Island of the Indonesian archipelago, many Cape slaves originated there. This letter is relevant to our present purpose insofar as it speaks of a deeply rooted Buginese identity and a sense of belonging together, no matter how this awareness is characterised in modern socio-political terms. The letter writer, a fifty-year-old slave at the Cape, September of Bougies, uses such expressions as 'our Buganese people', 'your Buganese race', 'your suffering Buganese compatriots', and rounds off his letter by an obvious reference to the Bougies homeland: 'the children who came from the places of Boeloe Boeloe and Sanja-c' (Appendix I Shell, 1997: 60-61).

A couple of other documents, also written in Buginese, are extant. One such letter refers to some Muslim prophets and was used as a charm by Buginese deserters in 1786 (Worden and Groenewald, 2005: 355-84). In another criminal case of 1786 against Augustus van de Caab et al., a letter that was actually used as a charm was produced as a proof of the criminal intention of the accused. The letter was written in Buginese, but the official documentation described it as being 'een Arrabische' letter, while the *sententie* said it was 'in Malay characters'. In all the surviving documents, Bengali writing was conspicuous by its absence.

Early in the twentieth century, some attempts were made to record Cape slaves' autobiographical stories. In 1910, a journalist working for the African People's Organization (APO) interviewed Katie Jacobs, a ninety-six-year-old resident of District Six in Cape Town and one of the oldest living ex-slaves. Katie Jacobs remembered the days of her manumission in 1834 and lucidly narrated them to her interviewer. The text of the interview carrying a picture of Katie Jacobs with her two grandchildren was published in *African People's Organization Newsletter* (Xmas Number, 1910) and reproduced by Nigel Worden et al. (1996: 88-91) and Robert Shell (1997: 311-12). Sadly, we do not know of a similar effort to record Bengali ex-slaves' life stories.

Yet, on the administrative level, there is no dearth of data. Professor Robert Shell speaks of the 1,000 running metres of shelf space of crime records in the *Rijksarchief* (Royal Archives) in The Hague pertaining to the period of 1652-1795 and 'the equally voluminous civil cases' of that time (1994: footnote 14; and p. 185, footnote 68). This is corroborated by some of the documents brought out by a recently floated organisation, TANAP. TANAP is a joint initiative of the Royal Dutch Archives and Leiden University to ensure the conservation of VOC documents worldwide and to make them available to interested people so that they can be used efficiently. One of the projects, *Inventories of the Orphan Chamber of the Cape Town Archives Repository* yields as many as 20,386 'results' pertaining to the period of 1673-1844 in response to a search for 'slave' *(http://databases.tanap.net/mooc/)*. Of these, an indeterminate number relates to first generation Bengali slaves. Many of these records are likely to generate further information on Bengali slaves in the Cape.

TANAP's initiative in digitising VOC papers and making them accessible online has made available a very large number of documents relating to Bengal. These run into 614 pages containing virtual reconstruction to the tune of 1215 kb of diaries and letters using Dutch as the medium.

Shell himself studied individually each slave transfer in a dataset, forming part of the inventory he prepared, with reference to thirty-three variables. A similar exercise was carried out drawing on the materials of another set, cross-tabulated with twenty variables. However, he admits that the records of transactions of sale 'cannot reveal the long-term symbolical and psychological impact of sale', adding ruefully '- of course—no records can' (Shell, 1994).

While the overall aim of the TANAP is the full transcription of the resolutions of the VOC at the Cape, a specialised project with the acronym TEPC (*Transcription of Estate Papers at the Cape of Good Hope*) has been launched to transcribe the inventories of the estates of deceased persons. The justification behind this new drive is that while the TANAP is concerned with the official side of the working of the VOC, TEPC is expected to throw light on the lives of ordinary people. Even on these counts, official sources can only tell us about the manifest administrative and financial aspects of the transactions and interactions in which Bengali slaves were involved. These mostly related to incidents and happenings that came to light through recorded infringements of the law. By their very nature, these tended to highlight the extreme situations that witnessed the deviations from the orthodoxy—the prevailing norms of the superordinate stratum. These were at best the negative side of the master-slave relationship. The slaves involved could hardly claim to speak for the whole slave population, just as the dispensers of justice were in no way representative of the dominant white society. One can only speculate about the unrecorded cases that are more likely to tell us in greater detail about the things that 'went off well' - the positive side.

Furthermore, the official account of an event that was recorded and stored in the archives (i.e. the document that later researchers are likely to use) was the paraphrased version of what a witness or the accused said in the court, often in a language other than English or Dutch. More often than not, slaves and non-European witnesses were afraid to speak the truth; at other times, they were not in a position to speak freely. Passing through the intermediary of court officials, these translated accounts in many cases did not actually portray what happened in reality, especially in terms of the perception of the slaves. They were, in the words of John Mason, 'twice interpreted, filtered through two official minds' (quoted by Cornell, 2000: 55).

A neglected aspect of Bengali slaves' incorporation into local society is the impact of the structure of slavery on individual cases. Much too often, we regard slavery as a static institution. This is patently not true. For one thing, slavery in the Cape was shaped by the socio-economic conditions of the host society. In addition, its structure owed its origin to the constitutional and administrative set-up created by the VOC, operating from the Netherlands and Batavia in Indonesia through local functionaries. One has just to look at the various legislative enactments and administrative measures taken by the VOC regime to realise the relevance of this statement.

Table 7 summarises certain important laws and administrative decisions and their impact on the organisation of slavery in the Cape with special reference to slaves brought from Bengal.[15]

Table 7: Laws and Administrative Measures: their Impact on Slavery (1621-1841)

Year	Legislative enactments	Administrative measures	Their impact on slavery in the cape
1621	Synod of Dordrecht		Baptised slaves should not be sold; boost to oceanic slave trade
1657	Granting of farms to Dutch free burghers; expanded availability of usable land led to increased demand for labour		Demand for forced labour increased; slave trade boosted up
1658		First ship carrying slaves arrives	Demand for labour partly satisfied
1700	First *placcaat* restricted importation of Eastern slaves to the Cape		Supply of Bengali slaves decreases

1717	VOC retains slavery as the main labour supply system	Boost to slave trade in general
1767	Abolition of importation of Asian male slaves to the Cape	Supply of Bengali slaves suffers
1787	*Placcaat* for abolition of importation of Asian male slaves to the Cape	
1791	Private enterprise permitted to participate in slave trade	Supply of slaves expanded
1808	External slave trade banned	Recruitment of overseas slaves stopped; demand for Cape-born slaves expanded
1811	Outbreak of smallpox in the Lodge	Decimation of slave population and increased demand for slaves
1834	Abolition of slavery; slaves become apprentices	Apprenticeship system partly and for a limited period kept supply of slaves at the acceptable level
1838	End of slave apprenticeship system	Adverse effect on supply of labour partly satisfied by increased local supply through 'creolisation'. Mission stations provided land to many freed slaves; however, this was extended only to those who were Christians
1841	Proclamation of Masters and Servants Ordinance aimed at regulating relations between employers and employees	By making 'desertion' a criminal offence, it tried to ensure steady labour supply

The table highlights only the administrative and legislative measures, i.e. some of the 'superstructural' elements of Cape society and their impact on a specific socio-economic institution, viz. slavery. However, discussion of the introduction of slavery anywhere, including the Cape, has to be related to the possible transformation of the pre-existing mode of production—the base—through the new institution. Some social scientists have suggested that the Cape between the mid-seventeenth and late nineteenth centuries was characterised by a slave mode of production. Several of them refer to Karl Marx as having offered the concept. It is true that in Marx's scheme of the evolution of socio-economic formations, slave society forms an important stage before the emergence of feudalism. But it is doubtful if the introduction of slavery in the Cape, being an extension of the nascent capitalism in Western Europe, can justifiably be compared to slave societies of Greece and Rome.

This is not the place to probe the issue in depth. But Orlando Patterson's point may be well taken in this context. Rejecting the thesis that Cape society embodied a slave mode of production, Patterson argued that a society can depend heavily on slave labour, and yet its economy may not show features that are indicative of a characteristic slave mode of production (1979: 48-49). 'Most workers in Washington, DC are women,' said Patterson, '(but) Washington does not have a female mode of production.'

Paradoxically, the dependence on slave labour was in the process of contributing to the rise of a 'rentier' class in the urbanised areas of Cape Town and its surroundings, who lived not off land but off the *koeli geld ('Coolie money')* as Ross so aptly remarked. The 'koeli geld' assumed different forms: the practice of letting out of slaves for hire for different operations, including fishing, construction of buildings such as a new church, harvesting, sale or exchange of stolen goods, and 'sponsored' beachcombing. This was thus another way devised by masters of exploiting the labour of slaves for enriching themselves, a kind of expropriation of the surplus value produced by slaves. How this practice would conceivably have developed in future with its impact on social stratification can at best be speculated and only as a 'counterfactual' prospect because with the abolition of slave trade and of slavery shortly afterwards, this trend came to an end.

Slaves, domestic helpers, and even those engaged in farming in the Cape were alienated from the existing means of production organised by way of semi-capitalistic farming and herding. Their knowledge and expertise, as would have been stressed by Rosa Luxemburg (cf. 2002) about a hundred years ago, were separated from the production process. Slavery cannot thus be said to have lent any distinguishing mark to the Cape economy as far as the forces of production are concerned. As regards the social relations of production, the existence of slaves did make the Cape economy distinctive; but all things considered, it still remained a capitalist economy in which the nascent bourgeoisie's appropriation of the surplus produced by the underclass was the engine of growth. This does not necessarily go against the fact that Cape slavery was more brutal than class exploitation elsewhere. 'The slave variant of capitalism', to quote Patterson again, 'is merely capitalism with its clothes off' (1979: 51). However, the position of Bengali slaves in this system was no different in these respects from that of slaves of other ethnic groups.

Sources

Reconstruction of a piece of history of any country focused on a small foreign community and after three and a half centuries is always a risky undertaking. The difficulty is compounded when we have to depend mostly on *official* records. As said above, hardly any account emanating from Cape slaves and their progeny is extant.

In our case, the sources are undoubtedly more treacherous as the story of what kind of world Bengali slaves made for themselves and others has remained a closed book and will probably never be written. However, one should not prejudge the issue. The amount of material available is massive. Painstaking study of this may help us reconstruct the world Bengali slaves made for themselves and Cape society as a whole.

I. Primary Sources

1. Oral traditions

    Some oral traditions on the institution of slavery in the Cape have been collected, e.g. the life story of Katie Jacobs (see above). They shed light on slavery at the Cape and what happened after its abolition. In Carohn Cornell's *Slaves at the Cape: A Guidebook for Beginner Researchers* (2000: University of the Western Cape), information about other initiatives is provided.

    Music forms a specialised form of oral traditions. Much that cannot be communicated normally may take a stylised form of message through music, both vocal and instrumental. This was particularly the case in the Cape—a fact that was commented upon by several visitors. Remnants of slave music still persist in contemporary Malay music in the Cape through lyrics of *'ghoemaliedijies'* (*'ghoema* songs' accompanied by the beatings of a hide-covered drum or *'ghoema'*) and *'klopse'* music, especially at the time of the annual Coon Carnival, conventionally celebrated by the Coloured community. Musical legacy of this sort cannot persist except with the active patronage of a stable community, which Bengali slaves lacked. This is the main reason why there is no musical component of oral traditions in the Cape that are relevant to Bengali slaves.

2. Slave legacy in Cape culture comprising architecture, house furnishing, dress, food, cooking, language, religion, and music

Under this heading, the items which have so far attracted major attention relate to house furnishing, including cooking utensils, dress, and furniture. Much of the material that throws light on Bengali slave owners' life style and social status was collected from inventories of estates of deceased Bengali free blacks and *Vendurollen* (records of public auction list). Valuable insight into the life style of Bengali free blacks can be obtained from the researches of Antonia Malan.

3. Historical archaeology sources

Archaeological sources are increasingly being tapped for gathering relevant information of the past. Excavations at the South African Cultural History Museum, the Slave Lodge, the Vergelegen slave lodge, and Simon van der Stel's estate in Somerset West have yielded considerable amount of data relating to the institution of slavery during the seventeenth and twentieth centuries. An interesting find at Vergelegen was the skeleton of a middle-aged woman. Scientific study of the skeleton, the coffin that contained it and other artefacts found indicate that she was probably brought as a young woman from a tropical country which could as well have been Bengal.

Historical archaeological investigations have additionally made it possible for researchers to gather data about the slaves of other ethnic groups from intensive examination of particular localities, e.g. an area named as *Masambiekvlei* in Pniel where Mozambican slaves and their descendants lived (Cornell, 2000: 8). Insofar as Bengali slaves were never settled in specific localities, such a strategy might not be useful for our purpose.

4. Another source of information about slavery in the Cape consists, in general, of the paintings (including portraits) and drawings that reflect the social life of the period. This is a legacy of a European tradition carried forward to southern Africa. The picture of the wealthy Storm family from the Village Museum of Stellenbosch showing Burgher members of the family in the forefront with an almost unrecognisable slave in the shadowy background is a case in point. Another, more patent and almost a caricature of the snobbishness of the Cape idle rich, is the pencil sketch of Hendrik Cloete smoking a long pipe at the card table, the long stem of the pipe held for him by a male uniformed slave.

5. Documentary sources

    The availability of materials on the theme of slavery, slave trade, its abolition, and aftermath in the Cape archives is remarkable. We can only try to give below an indication of the major sources.

    5.1 The Cape Town Archives

    Court of Justice records, including minutes of the proceedings of the court, other documents detailing the names of the persons involved in a case, testimonies given, and the sentences, and records of interrogation.

    These materials are not available in English except those that have been translated for private or public use. A recent initiative in this regard resulted in a jointly edited volume, Nigel Worden and Gerald Groenewald (Eds.) (2005) *Trials of Slavery: Selected Documents Concerning Slaves from the Criminal Records of the Council of Justice at the Cape of Good Hope, 1705-1794*, published by the Van Reinbeck Society in Cape Town. This volume contains eighty-seven criminal records in Dutch original with their English translations, including twenty-six documents that concern Bengali slaves.

    There are other useful papers. For example, documents of the *Orphan Chamber* may prove their worth in reconstructing the history of slavery in the Cape. The *Orphan Chamber* was an institution set up in the seventeenth century for the protection of the interests of all free orphans, more specifically, for the administration of the property of persons who died intestate or left heirs who were under age or were not available locally.

Inventories of estates of deceased Bengali free blacks yield valuable information on their financial position, while the protector of slaves submitted reports that contained useful information about how slaves were treated in actuality. Records of purchases by them at public auctions are equally important sources. Some researchers have studied such records on the same person over the years for constructing a dynamic picture of a purchaser's fortune, e.g. Tracey Randle, 'Patterns of Consumption at Auctions: a Case Study of Three Estates', paper presented at the conference on the theme 'Contingent Lives: Social Identity and Material Culture in the VOC World'. Cape Town, December 2006.

Vendurollen (records of public auction list)

A *venduroll* is a list of all the goods (including slaves) sold at an auction. For every transaction, the names of slaves sold with the names of buyers and the prices paid for each slave were provided.

Opgaafrollen (census records)

Ahead of their times, the VOC organised annual censuses of the areas under their control. The *Opgaafrollen* give the number of slaves in each household, including their gender and age, but do not mention their names.

The Cape Town Archives contain a number of documents regarding various aspects of slavery and slave life in the Cape, especially after 1816. These also include returns of slaves furnished by owners, rules and regulations regarding slavery, information about casualties, and births, deaths, transfers, etc. kept in the slave registry office, mortgages, bonds, and deeds of transfer and vouchers of sale. Then there is a list of returns of slaves sold by public auction with the amount of each sale, return of slaves sold by private contract, power of attorney deeds for sale of slaves, deeds of manumission, minutes of proceedings of slave compensation office, documents regarding emancipation compensation claims, and receipts for compensation claims paid.

Then there are property records, preserved in the so-called Deeds Office. Included in these records are the wills and testaments (under

Masters of the Orphan Chamber (MOOC) series 7/1), Court of Justice records in civil and criminal cases (CJ series), and shipping records and diaries kept by ships' captains.

From the materials of the Cape Town Archives, the present writer prepared two lists of 267 documents, each of which carries the names of male and female Bengali slaves. The documents dealt with diverse subjects: will, '*vonnis*' (punishment verdict by a court), testament, request for manumission and emancipation of slaves, purchase and transfer of slaves, death notice, inventories of property, request for remission of fines and other penalties for various offences, request for exemption from payment of taxes, request for liquidation, and notarial protocols of different kinds, including requests for grant of power of attorney and mortgage deed. A few comprised requests for return to Bengal made either by the owner or the manumitted slave. An example of this phenomenon is the request made by Lady Campbell in 1823 in respect of Abdula, 'a free black'.

The Bengalis mentioned in these documents are variously characterised, depending on their positions and as perceived by the recorders such as 'slaves', 'freed slaves', and 'freed slave women'; 'free blacks'; 'free persons'; 'free men'; and 'servants' (1840), 'coolies' (1845), and 'game sellers'. This at once reflected the muddled official mind and provided a further source of confusion for future researchers.

5.2 Other archives

Archives maintained by various churches, e.g. the Dutch Reformed Church, The Moravian Church, and the South African Missionary, among other groups.

Archiven van de Hoge Regering te Batavia (Archives of the High Government Batavia)

India Office Records (British Library, London)
National Archives at Kew Gardens, London
Stellenbosch Village Museum: papers and pictures

5.3 Reports, articles, and editorials in contemporary journals, e.g. *Cape Times* (weekly), *New Monthly Magazine*, South African Library, *South African Commercial Advertiser* (said to be the Cape Colony's first newspaper), and *South African Historical Journal*. Beginning with the 1820s, the Cape witnessed the emergence of private newspapers. These contained advertisements of slave auctions as well as rewards for help in capturing runaway slaves. Reports of public debates concerning slavery were also published in these papers.

5.4 In recent years, there has been a marked revival of community history writing in South Africa. There are laboriously produced inventories of Cape inhabitants of German origin; mixed marriages between Europeans, Coloureds, and Africans (Heese, *Groep sonder Grense*); and detailed genealogies of whites of the Cape (*Suid-Afrikaanse Geslagsregisters* or *South African Genealogies A-N*). For other genealogical details, old files of the *Kronos* (*Journal of Cape History*), *Capensis*, and *Familia* (*Journal of the South African Genealogical Society*) may be consulted. *The Cape Almanac* is also likely to prove to be an important source of family history and connection.

5.5 Theses and Dissertations

A large number of researches have been carried out in universities in South Africa and other countries. A few of them, not published in book form, proved useful in the preparation of the present monograph.

Bank, A. (1991). *Slavery in Cape Town, 1806-1834*. MA thesis. University of Cape Town: Department of History. Esp. Appendix 8: Inventory of Free Black Slave owners Identifiable by Name, Cape Town and Cape District, 1816-1834.

Davids, A. (1991). 'The Afrikaans of the Cape Muslims from 1815 to 1915'. University of Natal, MA thesis.

Rugarli, Anna Maria (1998). 'Slavery at the Cape Colony from Acquisition to the Process of Creolization, c. 1790-1830'. Thesis submitted to the Faculty of Political Sciences of the Universita' degli Studi, Milan, Italy. <www.club.it/culture/culture2001/anna.maria. rugarli/bibliographia.rugarli/corpo.tx.rugarlihtml>.

6. Private papers

Among documents that throw light on the institution of slavery at the Cape are Hendrik Cloete's private papers concerning his farm, *Groot*

Constantia. Cloete is known to have kept detailed records of the expenses he incurred on keeping his farm, including the cost of the board and lodging of his slaves and the money spent on their dress. These being part of his investment on the farm, Cloete kept account of how much money he spent on the farm and how much dividend he earned from it.

7. Cross-national sources, comprising archival materials and visual sources

7.1 Included in this category is an ambitious programme of a recently floated organisation, TANAP. The inventories of the MOOC, together with the minutes of the meetings of the Council of Policy, have been transcribed through its auspices and are now available online. Most of these are in old-style Dutch, but the inventories of MOOC are in English from the 1820s onwards. While the overall aim of the TANAP is the full transcription of the resolutions of the VOC at the Cape, a specialised project with the acronym TEPC has been launched to transcribe the inventories of deceased estates. The justification behind this new drive is that while the TANAP is concerned with the official side of the working of the VOC, TEPC is expected to throw light on the lives of ordinary people.

7.2 Mention should also be made of a recent initiative launched by various Dutch universities, academies and learned societies, archives, and museums to prepare a 'master' inventory of various visual materials (including maps, drawings, prints, and paintings of locations relating to the VOC that are available in different countries. Its mission statement and a complete list of sources accessed so far may be found on their website <*www.atlasofmutualheritage.nl*>. The inventory comprises several maps of Hooghly and Kasimbazar, a painting detailing the battle of the Nabab of Dacca in 1742 and a copy of a painting '*Arakanese pirates selling Bengali slaves at Pipli*', (cf. Appendix G) which may be of special interest to our readers.

II. Primary Asian Sources

Reference has been made above to the likely sources of data on the theme of slave trade between Bengal and other territories then occupied by the Dutch and other European powers. The present author has come across several such sources.

First, there are oral traditions of the ravage perpetrated by Mogh freebooters leading to desolation of the entire countryside of south Bengal and the abduction of Bengalis to be sold as slaves in Hooghly, Tamluk, and Chittagong in Bengal that included the presentday Bangladesh. A popular verse detailing the devastation caused by pirates of diverse European nationalities runs as follows:

নশিায় চলে না নৌোকা হার্মাদরে ডরে ।
তীর হইতে ওলন্দাজ ধনপেরাণে মারে ॥
ফরিঙ্গিগিরা কুলবতী নারী লইয়া যায় ।
ইংরাজ অঙ্গবঙ্গে সব লুটিয়া খায় ॥

'Boats do not ply at night due to fear caused by the Portuguese.
The Dutch kill everybody and loot their property from the shore.
The French on their part abduct women of respectable families,
While the English plunder everything of value in Bengal.'

Bengali slaves were often carried to markets outside of contemporary Bengal such as Pipli (in present-day Orissa) and Arakan (in Myanmar). We have come across some visual representations of this (see copy of a painting *Arakanese pirates selling Bengali slaves at Pipli*' reproduced as Appendix G of this monograph). A roughly written summary of these operations is provided in Jamini Mohan Ghose's *Magh Raiders in Bengal* published by Bookland in Calcutta in 1960 and Arasaratnam's long essay 'Slave Trade in the Indian Ocean' in K.S. Mathew, ed. *Mariners, Merchants and Oceans* (New Delhi, 1995).

Jamini Mohan Ghose also draws our attention to the importance, among other things, of genealogical records (*kula-panji*s and *kula-biboroni*s) of important lineages of Bengali society, belonging to such upper castes as Brahmans, Kayasthas, and Baidyas. According to him, many such accounts were recorded in Sanskrit, often untutored and in Bengali scripts. These genealogical records were kept for generations in family strongboxes and even more securely in the private custody of family matchmakers (*ghatak*s) for obvious reasons. Ghose himself quoted some such documents which reveal the names of certain Bengali maidens from upper-caste (and upper-class) families. These were abducted by Mogh pirates, sometimes working *in tandem* with Portuguese freebooters.

One such specimen is reproduced below (as quoted by Sen, 2006: Introduction, p. 7):

ততঃ সুরূপা-মণিরূপা-কর্পূরমঞ্জরী এতাঃ কন্যা মঘনে নীতা

'Thus beautiful maidens such as Manirupa and Karpurmanjari were abducted by the Moghs.'

The spread of the Mogh-Portuguese network is also seen from the following excerpt, cited by Ghose (p. 33), taken from one of the genealogical records, of which the full reference is unfortunately missing:

রামশরণস্য সত্রুী হরহিরস্য কন্যা মঘনে নীতা পপিপলী বন্দরে বিবাহিতা । সা কন্যা শান্তপিুরে আগতা রামশরণ গৃহে । রামশরণনে গর্ভ কৃতঃ সা মাট্টিারতিে স্থথিতা ।

> 'Harihara's daughter and Ramsaran's wife was abducted by the Moghs, taken to the port of Pipli, and married off there. This lady returned to Ramsaran's home at Shantipur. Impregnated by Ramsaran, she went again to Matiari and stayed there.'

The extent of the dread that Moghs generated locally can be gauged by such expressions as *Mogher muluk* (disorderly and lawless state of affairs in a territory dominated by Moghs), still current in colloquial Bengali. Also Hindu puritans would at that time refer to *Mogh dosha* to mean a special type of bodily pollution caused to people who came into 'unholy' contact with Moghs. And if a community was thus dishonoured as a whole, it would bear the degrading adjective of *Mougha* indefinitely (thus, *Mougha Brahmana, Mougha Kayastha*, etc.)

It is known that Portuguese adventurers were close associates of Mogh pirates and that the Mughal administration based in Delhi fought for a long time to rid the Gangetic delta of the Mogh-Portuguese menace. Piracy in the region often leading to some form of slavery, however, continued even after the Mughal conquest of Hooghly in 1635. In fact, there were new entrants in the stage: the Dutch and the English. There is evidence that some of the slaves the pirates abducted in this area were taken to Batavia and even to the Cape. According to Arasaratnam, at one stage, Mughal officials accused the VOC authorities of transporting 5,000-6,000 Bengalis per year as slaves to Batavia. These were said to have been kidnapped by the Arakanese slavers in southern Bengal (Ghose, 1960: 204).

Another potential source for historical reconstruction of kinship relations among Hindus takes us to records kept by the *panda*s of Gaya, about 250 miles from Calcutta. Pandas are priests who organise rituals of offerings of 'libation' (*pinda*s) by pilgrims to their ancestors on the sacred banks of the Phalgu (or Falgu) River near Gaya. Such records are stored for generations with sundry details of the persons concerned and could reveal some of the missing links in the family trees of pilgrims. Thanks to such information, the researcher is likely to be in a better position to throw light on the social history of the lower Gangetic delta devastated by Mogh and Portuguese marauders and later by adventurers of other nations.

Additionally government archives in countries such as India, Bangladesh, and Indonesia, and possibly also Myanmar have some materials on slave trade in different languages. A paper read by Anjana Singh of the University of Leiden at the conference on the theme 'Contingent Lives: Social Identity and Material Culture in the VOC World'. Cape Town, December 2006 ('From Amsterdam via Batavia to Cochin: mid-eighteenth Century Individuals and Institutions of the VOC') carries some useful information in this regard.

III. Web Sites

André van Rensburg website: *My Genetic Enrichment: Slaves at the Cape, South Africa* Tandre@rensburg.com.

Iziko: Museums of Cape town 'Heritage of Slavery in South Africa Slavery at the Cape' <http://www.iziko.org.za/sh/resources/slavery/slavery.html>.

South Africa's Stamouers <www.stamouers.com>.

IV. Secondary Sources

Achmat, Davids (1989). 'The Words Slaves Made'. Paper presented at the conference on the theme *Cape Slavery and After*, 10-11 August 1989, Organized by the Department of History, University of Cape Town. Also published as an article with the same title in the South African Journal of Linguistics, 1985.

Arasaratnam, Sinnappah (1995). 'The Slave Trade in the Indian Ocean in the Seventeenth Century' in K. S. Mathew, (Ed.). *Mariners, Merchants and Oceans: Studies in Maritime History*. Manohar Publications: New Delhi,

Armstrong, Therese (2008). *From Rags to Riches*. An online document ('Rags to Riches [1].doc') kindly made available to the present author by Mrs Armstrong on 18 July 2008, theresebenade@mac.com.

Banglapedia: National Encyclopedia of Bangladesh. Articles on Ostend Company.

Benadé, Therese (2005). *Kites of Good Fortune*. Cape Town: David Philip and New Africa Books (Afrikaans translation, *Anna, Dogter van Angela van Bengale*. David Philip).

Blussé, L. and F. Glaastra (1981). *Companies and Trade*. Leiden University Press.

Böeseken, Anna (1977). *Slaves and Free Blacks at the Cape, 1658-1700*. Cape Town: Tafelberg. Esp. *Addendum 2: A Brief Summary of Transactions Pertaining to Slavers, compiled from Documents Preserved in the Deeds Office, Cape Town*, pp. 121-94.

Boxer, C. R. (1965). *The Dutch Sea-borne Empire 1600-1800*. London: Hutchinson.

Bradlow, Frank R. Margaret Cairns (1978). *The Early Cape Muslims: A Study of their Mosques, Genealogy and Origins*. Cape Town: A. A. Balkema.

Brink, André (1982/Penguin 1983). *A Chain of Voices*. New York: Penguin.

Chanana, Dev Raj (1995). *Prachin Bharate Das Protha*. Kolkata: K.P. Bagchi. This book is a Bengali translation of Chanana's *Slavery in Ancient India* (Bombay: People's Publishing House, 1960). The English work is based on the author's doctoral thesis submitted to the University of Paris and later published in French under the title *L'esclavage dans l'Inde ancienne après les texts Palis et Sanskrits* by the Institut Francais d'Indologie in Pondichery in 1957.

Chatterjee, Indrani and Richard M. Eaton (Eds.) (2006). *Slavery and South Asian History*. Bloomington and Indianapolis, IN: Indiana University Press.

Chatterji, Suniti Kumar (1968; reprint 2004). *India and Ethiopia: From the Seventh Century B.C.* Kolkata: The Asiatic Society.

Chowdhury, Fatima (November 20, 2005). 'India's African Past'. Available from: http://www.boloji.com/wfs4/wfs492.htm.

Chowdhury, Sushil (1975). *Trade and Commercial Organizations in Bengal, 1650-1720*. Calcutta: Firma K.L. Mukhopadadhyay.

Chowdhury, Sushil (1995). *From Prosperity to Decline—Eighteenth Century Bengal, 1650-1720*. New Delhi: Manohar.

Coetzee, Carli (1998). 'Krotoa Remembered: A Mother of Unity, a Mother of Sorrows?' in Sarah Nuttal and Carli Coetzee (Eds.) (1998). *Negotiating the Past: The Making of Memory in South Africa.* Cape Town: Oxford University Press Southern Africa.

Cornell, Carohn (1998-99). 'Whatever Became of Cape Slavery in Western Cape Museums?' *Kronos*, No. 25, pp. 259-79.

Cornell, Carohn (2000). *Slaves at the Cape: A Guidebook for Beginner Researchers.* Bellville: University of the Western Cape, History Department, Slavery and Heritage Project.

Dange, S. A. (1949). *India: From Primitive Communism to Slavery.* Bombay: People's Publishing House.

Das Gupta, Ashin (1979). *Indian Merchants and the Decline of Surat c. 1700-1750.* Wiesbaden: Franz Steiner Verlag.

Dasgupta, Biplab (2000). 'Trade in Pre-colonial Bengal', *Social Scientist*, Vol. 28, Nos. 5-6, pp. 324-25.

Davids, A. (1990). 'The Words the Slaves Made: A Socio-Historical-Linguistic Study', *South African Journal of Linguistics*, Vol. 8, No. 1. pp 1-24.

Davids, A. (1991). 'The Afrikaans of the Cape Muslims from 1815 to 1915', MA thesis, University of Natal.

Dooling, Wayne. (1992) Law and Community in a slave society: Stellenbosch District, South Africa, c. 1760-1820. Cape Town, Centre for African Studies, University of Cape Town. Communications No. 23.

Eaton, Richard M. (1993). *The Rise of Islam and the Bengal Frontier, 1204-1760.* Berkeley: University of California Press. Available from: http://ark.cdlib. org/ark:/13030/ft067n99v9/. eGenealogical Society of South Africa (2005). *Monsterrol van de Vrije Luijden Opgemaaket, 23 January 1702* (Muster roll of the Free Settlers Compiled 23 January 1702) <eGGSA/ eGSSA>. eGenealogical Society of South Africa (2005). *Genealogy without Frontiers.* Compiled by Richard Ball. Available from: <www.eggsa.org/ transcriptions/monsterrollen/1702/mr_1702_intro.htm.>

Elphick, R. and H. Giliomee (Eds.) (1989). *The Shaping of South African Society, 1652-1840*. Cape Town: Wesleyan.

Faasen, Kobus, 'Education during the DEIC (Dutch East India Company or VOC) period 1652-1795' in TEPC (2006). *The Inventories of the Orphan Chamber of the Cape of Good Hope* (p. 18). Paper submitted to the conference on the theme Contingent Lives: Social Identity and Material Culture in the VOC World. Cape Town, December 2006.

Feldbaek, Ole (1991). 'No Ship for Tranquebar for 25 Years, Or the Art of Survival of a Mid-17th Century European Settlement in India' in Roderich Ptak and Dietmar Rothermund (Eds.) *Emporia, Commodities and Entrepreneurs in Asian Maritime Trade c. 1400-1750*. Stuttgart: Franz Steiner Verlag.

Genovese, Eugene D. (1976). *Roll, Jordan Roll: The World the Slaves Made*. New York: Vintage Books.

Ghose, Jamini Mohan (1960). *Magh Raiders in Bengal*. Calcutta: Bookland.

Gerald Groenewald (2006) *Panaij van Boegies*: slave—bandiet—caffer', in: Robert Shell (ed.), *From Diaspora to Diorama: The Slave Lodge in Cape Town, 1658 to 1828* Cape Town, 2006, pp. 595-614.

Hattingh, J. L. (1980). 'Die Blanke Nageslag van Louis van Bengale en Lijsbeth van die Kaap,' *Kronos*, Vol. 3 (Transactions of the Western Cape Institute for Historical Research, University of the Western Cape), pp. 5-51.

Hattingh, J. L. (1981). 'Louis van Bengalen', *Die Eerste Vryswartes van Stellenbosch, 1679-1720*, University of the Western Cape, Bellville.

Hattingh, J. L. (1981). 'Slawevrystellings aan die Kaap tussen 1700 en 1720', *Kronos*, Vol. 4, pp. 24-37.

Heese, H. F. (1981). 'Slawegesinne in die Wes-Kaap, 1665-1795', *Kronos* (Transactions of the Western Cape Institute for Historical Research, University of the Western Cape), Vol. 4.

Heese, Hans Friedrich (1984). *Groep sonder Grense: Die rol en status van de gemengde bevolking aan die Kaap, 1652-1795*. Bellville: Wes Kaaplandse Instituut vir Historiese Navorsing (in Afrikaans).

Hesse, J. A. and R. T. J. Lombard (1986). *Suid-Afrikaanse Geslagsregisters/South African Genealogies A-N.* Pretoria: Human Sciences Research Council.

Jayaram, N. (Ed.) (2004). *The Indian Diaspora: Dynamics of Migration.* New Delhi: Sage.

Joyce, Peter (1989). *The South African Family Encyclopedia.* Cape Town: Struik Publishers.

Kaarsholm, Preben (2008). 'Migration, Islam and Identity in Kwazulu-Natal: Notes on the Making of Indians and Africans'. Paper presented at a seminar organised by the Institute of Development Studies, Calcutta, on 4 February 2008.

Langham-Carter, R. (1985). 'The Slaves of Protea (Bishopscourt)', *Cabo (Journal of the Historical Society of Cape Town)*, Vol. 3, No. 4.

Liebenburg, H. (2003). *Introduction to Resolutions of the Council of Policy of the Cape of Good Hope.* Internet publication of the TANAP project. Available from: <www.tanap.net>.

Lombard, R. T. J.1984. *Handbook for Genealogical Research in South Africa. Pretoria, Human Science Research Council, Institute for Historical Research,*

Long, the Rev. James (original ed. 1850 published in the *Journal of Royal Asiatic Society of Bengal*; reprinted by the Beer Press in 1923 in Agartala, Tripura, India; second reprint published by the Tripura State Tribal Cultural Research Institute and Museum). *Analysis of Rajmala or Chronicles of Tripura.*

Luxembourg, Rosa (2002). 'Slavery' in Peter Hudis and Kevin B. Anderson (Eds.). *The Rosa Luxemburg Reader.* Kharagpur: Cornerstone Publications. This manuscript, came to light in the 1990s and was first published in the 2002 issue of the *Jahrbuch für Historische Kommunismusforschung* edited by *Narihiko Ito*, a well-known researcher who worked on the life and times of Rosa Luxemburg.

Malan, Antonia (Compiler)2008 *Index of Vendurollen (Auction Lists).* Cape Archives: MOOC (Maser of Orphan Chambers) probate documents, 10/1/1.

Malan, Antonia (1998-99). 'Chattels or Colonists? 'Freeblack' Women and Their Households', *Kronos*, Vol. 25, Pre-Millennium issue, pp. 50-71.

Malherbe, J. E. (1998). *The Edict of Nantes, 1598-1998: Four Hundred Years.* History Series No. 3. Franschhoek: Huguenot Memorial Museum.

Malherbe, Vertrees C. (2006) 'Illegitimacy and Family Formation in Colonial Cape Town, to c.1850'. Journal of Social History. Vol. 39, No.4, pp.1153-1176.

Mansell, G. Upham (forthcoming). *Consecrations to God: The Nasty, Brutish and Short Life of SUSANNA from Bengal, otherwise known as ONE EAR: The Cape of Good Hope's 2nd Recorded Female Convict, CAPENSIS.*

Marais, Johannes Stephanus (first published in 1939; republished in 1968). *The Cape Coloured People, 1652-1837.* Johannesburg: Witwatersrand University Press.

Mason, J. (1990). 'Hendrik Albertus and His Ex-Slave Mey: A Drama in Three Acts', *Journal of African History*, Vol. 31, pp. 423-45.

Mason, John Edwin (1999). '"Some Religion He Must Have": Slaves, Sufism, and Conversion to Islam at the Cape'. Paper read at the Southeastern Regional Seminar in African Studies (SERSAS), Savannah, GA.

Mason, John Edwin (2003). *Social Death and Resurrection of Slavery and Emancipation in South Africa.* Charlottesville: University of Virginia Press.

Mentzel, Otto Friedrich (originally published in German in three volumes in 1785-87; English translation by G. V. Marais and J. Hoge; revised and edited with an introduction by H. J. Mandelbrote). *A Complete and Authentic Geographical and Topographical Description of the Famous and All Things Considered Remarkable African Cape of Good Hope.* Cape Town: Van Riebeeck Society, 1921, 1925, 1944.

Newton-King, Susan (2006), 'Sodomy, Race and Respectability in Stellenbosch, 1689-1762: The Story of a Family Loosely Defined' in TEPC (2006). *The Inventories of the Orphan Chamber of the Cape of Good Hope* (p. 18). Paper presented at the conference on the theme *Contingent Lives: Social Identity and Material Culture in the VOC World.* Cape Town, December 2006.

Pankhurst, Richard (2000). 'History of the Ethiopian Diaspora 1: Ethiopians in Ancient and Early Medieval Times'. Available from: <http:// addistribune. com/Archives/2000/03/31-03-00/Hist.htm>

Patterson, Orlando (1979). 'On Slavery and Slave Formations', *New Left Review*, Vol. 117, Sep.-Oct., pp. 31-67.

Prakash, Om (1984). *Dutch Factories in India, 1617-1627*. Manohar Publishers and Distributors: Delhi.

Prakash, Om (1985). *The Dutch East India Company and the Economy of Bengal, 1630-1720*. Princeton, NJ: Princeton University Press.

Randle, Tracy (2006). 'Patterns of Consumption at Auctions: A Case Study of Three Auctions' in TEPC (2006). *The Inventories of the Orphan Chamber of the Cape of Good Hope* (p. 18). Paper presented at the conference on the theme *Contingent Lives: Social Identity and Material Culture in the VOC World*. Cape Town, December 2006.

Ray, Aniruddha (1998). *Adventurers, Landowners and Rebels, Bengal c. 1575-c. 1715*. Delhi: Munshiram Mahoharlal.

Raychaudhuri, Tapan (1962). *Jan Company in Coromandel, 1605-1690*. The Hague: Martinus Nijhoff.

Raychaudhuri, T. and I. Habib (Eds.) (1982). *The Cambridge Economic History of India: c.1200-1750*, Vol. 1. Cambridge University Press: New York, pp. 30-32, 92-93, and 530. Riebeeck, van Jan Antonisz (1952-57). *Daghregister gehouden by den oppercoopman, Jan Antonisz van Riebeeck (Journal of Jan van Riebeeck)*. 3 vols.

D. B. Bosman and H. B. Thom (Eds.). Cape Town: Balkema. The English translation of this work, edited by H. B. Thom, was published for the Van

Riebeeck Society in 1954 by A. A. Balkema, Cape Town and Amsterdam.

Ross, Robert (1983). *Cape of Torments: Slavery and Resistance in South Africa*. London: Routledge & Kegan Paul.

Rugarli, Anna Maria (1998). 'Slavery at the Cape Colony from Acquisition to the Process of Creolization, c. 1790-1830', Thesis presented at the Faculty of Political Sciences of the Universita' degli Studi, Milan, Italy.

Sarah, Nuttall and Carli Coetzee (Eds.) (1999). *Negotiating the Past: The Making of Memory in South Africa*. Oxford: Oxford University Press.

Schoeman, Karel (2007). *Early Slavery at the Cape of Good Hope, 1652-1717.* Pretoria: Protea Book House.

Sen, Abhijit (2006). *Mousumi Samudrer Upakule* (historical fiction in Bengali, *On the Coasts Served by the Monsoons.* Kolkata: Gangchil).

Shell, Robert C.-H. (first printed in 1994; reprinted in 1997). *Children of Bondage: A Social History of the Slave Society at the Cape of Good Hope, 1652-1838.* Johannesburg: Witwatersrand University Press.

Shell, Robert C.-H. (Compiler) (2008). *Diaspora to Diorama: The Old Slave Lodge in Cape Town.* On CD-ROM. Cape Town: Ancestry 24.

Singh, Anjana (2006). 'From Amsterdam via Batavia to Cochin: Mid-Eighteenth Century Individuals and Institutions of the VOC'. Paper read at the conference on the theme *Contingent Lives: Social Identity and Material Culture in the VOC World.* Cape Town, December 2006.

Sinha, Narendra Krishna (1956 and 1962). *The Economic History of Bengal: From Plassey to the Permanent Settlement.* Vol. 1 (1956) Calcutta: Published by the Author. Vol. 2 (1962) Calcutta: Firma K. L. Mukhopadhyay.

Skotnes, Pippa (Ed.) (1996). *Miscast: Negotiating the Presence of the Bushmen.* Cape Town: University of Cape Town Press.

Subramanyam, Sanjay (1990). *The Political Economy of Commerce.* Cambridge: Cambridge University Press.

Vaughan, Megan (2005) *Creating the Creole Island: Slavery in Eighteenth-Century Mauritius* by. Duke University Press.

Tinker, Hugh (1993) *A New System of Slavery: The Export of Indian Labour Overseas, 1830-1920.* London: Hansib Publishing Limited. 1st ed. Oxford University Press in 1974

Todescini, Fabio (2003). 'Some Reflections on Place, Tangible and Intangible Heritage and on Identity Construction'. International Council on Monuments and Sites (ICOMOS): Conference in Victoria Falls 2003.

Tripathi, Amales (1956). *Trade and Finance in the Bengal Presidency (1793-1833).* Calcutta: Orient Longmans.

Van der Merwe, Matthijs P. S. (1997). *Groot Constantia, 1685-1885: Its Owners and Occupants*. Cape Town: South African Cultural History Museum.

Van Gelder, Roelof (2006). 'Letters, Journals and Seeds: Forgotten Dutch Mail in the National Archives in London' (p. 4). Paper presented at the conference on the theme *Contingent Lives: Social Identity and Material Culture in the VOC World*. Cape Town, December 2006.

Van Kessel, Ineke (2006). 'Goa Conference on the African Diaspora in Asia', *African Affairs*, Vol. 105, No. 420, pp 461-464.

Van Leur, J. C. (1955). *Indonesian Trade and Society*. The Hague: W. Van Hoeve.

Vink, Markus P. M. (2006). '"A Work of Compassion?" Dutch Slavery and Slave Trade in the Indian Ocean in the Seventeenth Century'. Paper presented at the conference on the theme *Contingent Lives: Social Identity and Material Culture in the VOC World*. Cape Town, December 2006.

Vink, Markus (2003). 'The World's Oldest Trade: Dutch Slavery and Slave Trade in the Indian Ocean in the Seventeenth Century', *Journal of World History*, Vol. 14, No. 2, pp 131-177. The History Cooperative.

Ward, Kerry (2006). 'Knocking on Death's Door: Mapping the Spectrums of Bondage and Status through Marking the Dead at the Cape'. Paper presented at the conference on the theme *Contingent Lives: Social Identity and Material Culture in the VOC World*. Cape Town, December 2006.

Ward, Kerry and Nigel Worden (1998). 'Commemorating, Suppressing, and Invoking Cape Slavery' in Sarah Nuttal and Carli Coetzee (Eds.). *Negotiating the Past: The Making of Memory in South Africa*. Cape Town: Oxford University Press,

West Bengal State Book Board (2000; 2nd reprint). *Collected Works of Haraprasad Shastri*, Vol. 2. Calcutta. Shastri made the statement quoted on p. 3 of this paper in his presidential address at the seventh Bengali Literary Conference held in Calcutta in 1913 (Bengali Era 1321).

Worden, N. A. (1982). 'Violence, Crime and Slavery on Cape Farmsteads in the Eighteenth Century', *Kronos*, Vol. 5, pp. 43-60.

Worden, Nigel (1985). *Slavery in Dutch South Africa*. Cambridge: Cambridge University Press.

Worden, Nigel and C. Crais (Eds.) (1994). *Breaking the Chains*. Johannesburg: Witwatersrand University Press.

Worden, Nigel and Gerald Groenewald (Eds.) (2005). *Trials of Slavery: Selected Documents Concerning Slaves from the Criminal Records of the Council of Justice at the Cape of Good Hope, 1705-1794*. Cape Town: Van Riebeeck Society.

Worden, Nigel with Ruth Versfeld, Dorothy Dyer and Claudia Bickford-Smith (1996). *The Chains that Bind Us: A History of Slavery at the Cape*. Cape Town: Juta.

Worden, Nigel, E. van Heyningen, and Claudia Bickford-Smith (1998). *Cape Town: The Making of a City*. Cape Town: David Philip.

C. Databases

Kerry Ward's database on *bandieten* (convicts)

Database of slave transactions in the Cape during 1658-1783.

D. Interviews and Personal communications

Interview with Antonia Malan, University of Cape Town Library, 23 December 2002

Interview with Jim Armstrong, Cape Town Archives, 2002

Interview with Robert C.-H. Shell at his residence, December 2002

Personal communications from Jim Armstrong

END NOTES

No. Terms

1. Siddi
2. TANAP
3. Sejarah Melayu
4. The Colebrooke and Bigge Commission
5. Free blacks
6. Khoisan status
7. The Heeren XVII
8. Age divisions among slaves
9. Mild domestic chastisement
10. Malay identity
11. Radja of Tamborah
12. Synod of Dordrecht
13. Tuan Guru
14. Use of non-European languages and scripts
15. Laws regarding slaves

Endnotes

1. Siddi

In a recent study, Richard Eaton (cf. Chatterjee and Eaton, 2006) narrates the rise and fall of the 'military slavery' of the Habshis, in the western Deccan between 1450 and 1650. He demonstrates the important role played by the Habshis in the Nizam Shahi court with special reference to Malik Ambar 'Chapu' (1548-1626). The markedly African character of the sultanate under Malik Ambar's 'rule' comes out clearly from his account. By the mid-seventeenth century, however, Ethiopian males have been absorbed into local society as native householders.

Some attempts are now being made to reconstruct the evolution and present position of different Siddi groups in India. A conference held in Goa, India, in January 2006 was a direct outcome of the floating of a cyber network called the TADIA (*The African Diaspora in Asia*). It brought out some hitherto unknown details of Sidi communities in India (Van Kessel, 2006: 461-64).

2. TANAP

An organisation named *Towards a New Age of Partnership* or TANAP was floated some years ago for the preservation and utilisation of the VOC archives in the three continents of Europe, Asia, and Africa and to study economic and social changes in Asia and southern Africa starting from the seventeenth century. It has been sponsored by a number of academic institutions based principally in the Netherlands. TANAP has sponsored some historical studies in India encouraging the following researchers to use VOC sources:

Ghulam Ahmad Nadri *Dutch Trade in Cutch-Mandavi in the 1750s*

Binu M. John Parambil *The Ali Rajas of Cannanore: Status and Identity at the Interface of Commercial and Political Expansion (1664-1722)*

Anjana Singh *From Merchant-Warriors to Landlords. The Changing Perceptions of the Dutch in Cochin (1663-1795)*

3. *Sejarah Melayu* ('the Malay annals')

Sejarah Melayu ('the Malay annals') is a historical work in elegant classical Malay prose that traces the establishment of the Malacca Sultanate and covers over six centuries of the Malay peninsula's history, including the advent and spread of Islam in the region. The manuscript is said to have been compiled on traditional paper in the early seventeenth century by the prime minister of the Royal Court of Johor. The book presents intricate details of royal protocol and royal dynasties, combining them with various historical, mythical, and legendary figures and episodes in a compendium that still captivates its audience.

4. Colebrooke and Bigge Commission

In 1823, Major William Colebrooke and John Thomas Bigge were appointed as members of a Royal Commission of Enquiry (popularly known as the Colebrooke and Bigge Commission) to report on slave trafficking in the Cape. In 1825, Achmat himself gave evidence before the commission to report on the 'native' inhabitants of southern Africa.

5. Free blacks (*vryswarts*)

A slave engaging in slave trade after gaining freedom is ironical. But it aptly illustrates the popular saying: 'If you can't beat them, join them.' The irony is compounded when a slave owner (formerly a slave himself or herself) inflicts severe physical punishment on his or her slaves. In the early days of Company administration, there is at least one such case on record when such a slave owner was originally from Bengal. Robert Shell (1994: 209) mentions the case of Robert Scott of Bengal who put chains on female slaves on his own. Scott was arraigned before the Fiscal on a complaint by his victims. Scott is said to have justified his action by claiming 'private authority'. Yet, records show that free blacks (seemingly including those originating from Bengal) had the distinction of freeing the largest number of slaves per capita (Shell, 1997: 389).

In this context, the status of 'free blacks' (*vryswart)* should be clarified. Free blacks were mostly former slaves of African and Asian origin who, on manumission, achieved this status. The category additionally included some Chinese convicts (called '*bandieten*') and a few political exiles, mainly from what today is Indonesia. In contemporary literature, they have been variously described.

Curiously, although legally free, free blacks suffered from certain disabilities. Even before manumission, some of them were subjected to the practice of *obsequium*, i.e. specific duties to the families who freed them. Such duties included showing deference and respect to them. If in financial trouble, the emancipators could expect support in cash from the manumitted slaves. Fortunately, only a small proportion of freed slaves were under such obligation contractually.

Manumitted slaves suffered in several other ways. Unlike burghers, they could not work for the Company. They did not obtain credit from public authorities even though they were obliged to pay taxes. Finally, after death, the estate of a freed slave went to his former owner. The VOC authorities, following Roman Dutch law, distinguished between a free person, i.e. a full citizen or burgher, and a freed person, i.e. a manumitted slave. Not all rights and privileges enjoyed by a burgher were automatically granted to a freed person.

It helps to distinguish between the status of the free blacks and that of the free burghers. The latter were of white Dutch (or European) and mostly Christian origin. Naturally, they could not be enslaved. They were allowed, or even encouraged, to own land. However, they were required to do military service and had to take an oath of loyalty to the States-General (i.e. the Dutch government) and the VOC. Yet they had no say in the administration of the colony. The VOC had the right to deport unwanted burghers from the colony.

6. Khoisan status

The status of the Khoisan was ambiguous. By law, they could not be enslaved. But they were not regarded as free labour. In all cases, they were bonded to the farm (and the master or mistress) for a fixed term that varied from case to case. For this, they received no cash payment but were provided with food and clothing. The main difference between Khoisan workers and slaves (of other ethnic groups) lay in the fact that, unlike the latter, the Khoisan labourers could not be bought and sold.

Autochthonous people (Khoisan) were subjected to a system characterised by Robert Shell as 'tenurial bondage' or Cape serfdom (Shell, 1997: 30). Under this arrangement, Khoi labourers were bonded to their workplace for a specific period and could be transferred to a new owner when the property changed hands. They were not paid for their labour. Interestingly, although this system was widely practiced, it was not supported by any law. The abolition of the oceanic slave trade in 1808 led to an extension of 'enserfment' of the Khoisan.

7. *The Heeren XVII*

The board of directors of VOC was often referred to as *the Heeren XVII* (in English, 'the Gentlemen Seventeen') in official documents. Some alternative designations were as follows: the 'Council of XVII, 'the XVII' and 'the Lords and Masters'. This body constituted the highest level of administration in the VOC.

Organisation

The VOC consisted of six chambers *(Kamers)* in port cities: Amsterdam, Delft, Rotterdam, Enkhuizen, Middelburg, and Hoorn. Delegates of these chambers convened as the *Heeren XVII* (the Lords Seventeen).

Of the *Heeren XVII*, eight delegates were from the Chamber of Amsterdam (one short of a majority on its own), four from the Chamber of Zeeland, and one from each of the smaller chambers, while the seventeenth seat was alternatively from the Chamber of Zeeland or rotated among the five small chambers. Amsterdam had thereby the decisive voice. The Zeelanders in particular had misgivings about this arrangement at the beginning. The fear was not unfounded, because in practice it meant Amsterdam stipulated what happened.

The six chambers raised the start-up capital of the Dutch East India Company:

Chamber	Capital (guilders)
Amsterdam	3,679,915
Zeeland	1,300,405
Enkhuizen	540,000
Delft	469,400
Hoorn	266,868
Rotterdam	173,000
Total	6,429,588

Of the early shareholders of the VOC, immigrants played an important role. Under the 1,143 tenderers were 39 Germans and no fewer than 301 Zuid-Nederlanders (roughly present Belgium and Luxemburg, then under Habsburg rule), of whom Isaäc le Maire was the largest subscriber with ƒ85,000. VOC's total capitalisation was ten times that of its British rival.

The logo of the VOC consisted of a large capital 'V' with an 'O' on the left and a 'C' on the right leg. The first letter of the hometown of the chamber conducting the operation was placed on top (see figure for example of the Amsterdam chamber logo). The flag of the company was orange, white, blue (see Dutch flag) with the company logo embroidered on it.

The *Heeren XVII* (Lords Seventeen) met alternately six years in Amsterdam and two years in Middelburg. They defined the VOC's general policy and divided the tasks among the Chambers. The chambers carried out all the necessary work, built their own ships and warehouses, and traded the merchandise. The *Heeren XVII* sent the ships' masters off with extensive instructions on the route to be navigated, prevailing winds, currents, shoals, and landmarks. The VOC also produced its own charts.

8. Age divisions among slaves

The age divisions used in these tables do not correspond to the measures of age employed by VOC administrators for Lodge residents. Officially, five age cohorts were used: sucklings (*suijgelingen*) (birth to 3 years), school children (*skoolkinderen*), boys and girls (*jongens en meijsies*, 4-16 and 4-14), maids (*meijdens*, 14 and above), and boys (*jongnes*, 16 and above).

9. Mild domestic chastisement

The practice before Lord Charles Somerset's proclamation in 1823 was to limit caning to a maximum of thirty-nine lashes. Now under the new order, the limit was reduced to twenty-five; in 1841, this was further lowered to fifteen. About the same time, slave owners were forbidden to flog female slaves. The flogging was to be done with rods or other instruments of domestic implements. Probably the most important proviso of this new order was to give slaves the right to lodge complaints at the offices of local magistrates when they thought that these rules were violated.

10. Malay identity

The attempted construction of a Malay identity drove a wedge among Cape Town inhabitants because it stressed the South-East Asian origin of the Cape Malays and the unifying bond of Islam among them. A negative consequence of this was to differentiate between the 'refined' Malay legacy and the miscegenation culture of the Coloured residents of the Cape. Many of the latter were Christians and born locally of mixed parentage, African and European. Interestingly, before and after freedom, Bengali slaves were assimilated into both these streams. As indicated above, some of them were incorporated into the white segment of the Cape population. Others gradually became a part of the Coloured community, while the remaining segment of the Bengali slave population was integrated into the general black community, comprising Khoikhoi, San, and Bantu people from South Africa and other regions of the Continent, and non-Bantu blacks from West Africa.

All these people were aware of the fact that their ancestral names (or surnames) had been impounded by colonial masters with the consequent loss of their distinctive history and identity. In the recent past, quite a few Cape Malays have been looking towards Indonesia to rediscover their roots. Others, including a number of Coloured people, have attempted to find their moorings in links with Khoisan peoples, generally regarded as the original inhabitants of the Cape. An extreme example of this took place in 1989 when the Pan-Africanist Congress leader, Benny Alexander, changed his name to '!KhoisanX', reminiscent of 'Malcolm X' in the USA. Evidently, this was to highlight his linkage to the indigenous inhabitants, rather than to slavery.

Comparing and contrasting the positions of the Malays and the Bengali slaves and their descendants in the Cape, it may be pointed out that the size of a group may not always be the sole determinant either of group cohesion or its contribution to society. This is clear when we contrast Bengali forced migration with voluntary migration of the Huguenots from France to the Cape. Both movements started in the seventeenth century. The first Huguenot arrival to the Cape took place in 1688, only about thirty years after the first Bengali slaves had been brought to the Cape. The exact number of Bengali immigrants to the Cape is not known; but it must have run into hundreds. The present author has made an inventory of Bengali slaves in the Cape between 1656 and 1834 from various sources, including archival materials. The list includes more than 700 slaves and Bengali *vryswart*s (free blacks). These were the first-generation Bengalis. It is very difficult to identify 'Bengalis' of later generations for reasons that have been detailed above (pp. 5-6). By contrast, according to a publication of the Huguenot Memorial Museum at Franschhoek, only about 270 Huguenots settled in the Cape during the seventeenth and early eighteenth centuries (*The Edict of Nantes 1598-1998*, compiled by J. E. Malherbe, p. 14). *The South African Family Encyclopaedia* (p. 173) puts the figure of Huguenots at 'about 300'.

Both communities have now been fully integrated into Cape society. Huguenots form part of the white Afrikaner community in the Cape via their settlement in the Drakenstein and Franschhoek areas dominated by Dutch and German free burghers. Descendants of Bengali slaves too are absorbed into various segments of local society. The Huguenot legacy can be seen in certain family names, e.g. De Villiers, Le Roux, Malan, Marais, and Du Toit. Bengali surnames were not used from the beginning; slaves from that region were given new personal names, mostly biblical. Surnames of the first-generation Bengalis were toponymic.

11. Radja of Tamborah

Several ex-kings and sultans from the Indonesian archipelago were banished in the Cape. Some of them were permitted to stay there with fairly large numbers of slaves to work for them. The Radja of Tamborah (original name, Abdul Bashir) was a valued representative of this group, but there were others such as Sheik Yusuf of Makassar. Sheikh Yusuf was a member of the royal house of Goa (in Indonesia) who was exiled to the Cape as a political prisoner by the VOC with a sizable entourage permitted to travel with him. He was later raised to the status of a Muslim saint. Ironically, in putting a religious coating on people like Sheikh Yusuf, their original status in Cape society was conveniently forgotten.

12. Synod of Dordtrecht

The Synod of Dordtrecht (1618-19), said to be the last meeting of Protestant theologians from Great Britain and the Continent, adopted certain clear-cut decisions bearing on slavery. These were as follows: (i) Lodge slaves must not be exchanged, sold, alienated, or exported. (ii) Slaves in the household, including the Lodge, had to be baptised and educated. (iii) They must be treated as ordinary servants. (iv) They must be paid a 'salary' known as *peculium*, paid mostly in kind at the Cape.

Dutch slave owners tried to get round this regulation in three ways, according to Shell (1997: 100): by (i) not baptising slaves, (ii) manumitting slaves on their deathbed, and (iii) transferring their slaves to a newly born child, a practice called *inter vivos*.

13. Tuan Guru

Tuan Guru (original name, Abdullah bin Kadi Abdus-Salaam), an exile from the Ternate Islands, and Sheikh Yusuf of Makassar, a member of the royal house of Goa, who was considered to have been a Muslim saint, cemented this bond. The string of mosques and tomb shrines (*keramat*s) of religious leaders in the Cape peninsula institutionalised it with considerable success.

Tuan Guru was imprisoned in the Robben Islands where he completed the manuscript of his famous book *Ma'rifah al-Islam wa al-Iman* ('Manifestations of Islam and Faith'). His release from prison in 1793 is regarded as a key event in the consolidation of the Islamic community of the Cape. Some scholars hold that the 'Ma'rifah' provided the ideological framework within which Muslim slaves and free blacks, many of whom were slave owners, could coexist and cofunction. The fact that Tuan Guru was himself a slave owner attaches special significance to this contribution. The importance of Tuan Guru as the spiritual *guru* of Cape Muslims is further heightened by the fact that he was instrumental in the creation of both the first madrasah and the first mosque at the Cape.

Haj Nurul Erfaan Rakiep, a descendant of Tuan Guru, is said to be the first 'Malay' South African to trace his Indonesian roots. His exploration took place in 1993 when he visited Tidore, an island in the Indonesian archipelago. Others followed him with similar mission.

14. Use of non-European languages and scripts

The minutes of the meeting of the Council of Policy of the Cape held on 27 March 1759 (C.137) contain a reference to certain problems arising out of the transfer of two Singhalese exiles, Leander de Saram and Louis Perera, from Stellenbosch to Swellendam. Later, the Council learnt about the letters that had been written in this connection in the language of the exiles, Singhalese, spoken in the southern part of present-day Sri Lanka (cf. 4.5.1761, C.139. TANAP, *Introduction to the Resolutions of the Council of Policy of Cape of Good Hope*). Unfortunately, the letters 'could neither be read nor understood by any VOC official'. Apparently no other person was found to help with the translation. The present author has found no further reference to the letters or to the use of the Singhalese language anywhere else in the Cape.

But there has been at least one case of a petitioner attaching his name in the Arabic characters to an official petition. This happened when Frans signed his name in Arabic alphabets in a memorandum that was forwarded to the Colebrooke-Bigge Commission. Interestingly, this event set out a trend that is suggestive of the growing popularity of 'Arabic-Afrikaans' or Afrikaans written in the Arabic script. Then there is the record of a Chinese free black called Quodjonko signing a deed of transfer of a slave in Chinese characters (Shell, 1997: 120; footnote 144).

As said above, there is no evidence of any slave communicating with any other person or agency or even signing a message or a document in his or her name in an Indian language (using an Indian script or even the Roman or Arabic script). To an extent, this may have been due to the widespread illiteracy prevalent at the time among Indian slaves (as also among slaves from other regions). Ironically, academic learning was not the strong point of the Burghers either. Quoting De Wet, Schoeman (p. 314) points out that, in the late seventeenth century, 'many of the white free burghers could barely trace a cross.'

15. Laws regarding slaves

The first legislation that changed considerably—at least formally—the legal position of slaves as chattels was issued on 26 April 1816. It made the registration of slaves compulsory, in order to distinguish them from the bulk of manumitted slaves and Prize Negroes. To this end, an office was established in Cape Town, managed by an inspector of the registry and an assistant inspector, who were in charge of registering against their masters' names the slaves' names, sex, age, place of origin, occupation, and any remarks concerning them.

This measure was later modified as part of a wider legislative initiative, Ordinance 19 of 19 June 1826, according to which a registrar and guardian of slaves was appointed to replace the inspector (and assistant guardians were appointed for the country districts as well). The guardian had the specific task of listening to slaves' complaints and investigating whether they were justified. In Ordinance 19, the relationship between masters and slaves was thoroughly regulated. Slave owners had to provide a certain amount of food daily and clothes yearly, they could not make slaves work more than what the law established, and they had to let them rest on Sundays. Moreover, masters could not sell slaves separately from their wives or children under the age of ten. Besides, slaves could testify under oath in courts, and their punishments were restricted to a maximum of twenty-five lashes for men and to a milder whipping on shoulders for women. Masters had also to instruct their slaves in the Christian faith in order to make them 'a more acceptable and politically safer subordinate class of labourers' (Rayner, 1981: 20; and Dooling, 1991: 75-94). Prior to this ordinance, there had been the Somerset Proclamation of 1823, whose measures, similar to these, were valid for baptised slaves only.

As underlined above, these legislative measures were conceived as steps in a long process after which slaves were supposed to be freed and automatically incorporated into society as a subordinate class of workers. Slavery was eventually abolished in 1838. Even after that, a freed slave was required to work as an apprentice of their former master for four years during which he had to look after him and his family and gradually earn his own livelihood and become independent. (Rugarli <www.club.it/culture/culture2001/anna.maria.rugarli/bibliographia. rugarli.html>

Appendices

Appendix A

Timeline of Slavery Involving Bengali Slaves in the Cape

31 December 1600 English East India Company founded

1602 Dutch East India Company (*Verenigde Oost-Indische Compagnie*) founded in the Netherlands

1621 Synod of Dordt banned sale of baptised slaves, announcing that they are to be treated as other Christians

1632 Mughal forces drove the Portuguese out of Hooghly

1635 Shahjahan's *farman* of 1 August permitted the Dutch to trade in Bengal from Hooghly

1652 Establishment of a refreshment outpost at the Cape by the VOC

1653 The first imported slave, Abraham van Batavia, i.e. originally from Batavia (now Jakarta in Indonesia), arrived at the Cape

1656 The first reference to a Bengali (manumitted) slave when Jan Woutersz, a soldier in the service of the VOC, married Catharina Anthonis, originally from Zalegon in Bengal

1657 Formal institution of 'free burghership' whereby farms were granted to Dutch free burghers

1658 Marriage (*banns*) between Jan Sacharias, a Dutch burgher, and Maria *van Bengalen*. The public notice was issued a fortnight before the marriage, and the subsequent marriage ceremony were recorded in the *daghregister* (journal) of Jan van Riebeeck

1658 First ship carrying slaves arrived at the Cape from West Africa; assisted European immigration to the Cape was allowed

1666 Slaves built the Cape Town Castle

1679 Start of the construction of the Company Slave Lodge

1688 The first slave revolt in Cape Town took place with the avowed aim of burning burghers' houses in the town. This was led by a free black Sante van Sante Jago of Cape Verde and a slave by the name of Michiel

1693 According to official figures, slaves at the Cape now outnumbered free population for the first time

1700 First *placcaat* restricted importation of Eastern slaves to the Cape

1706 Burgher revolt in the Cape that led to the end of the Van der Stel dynasty

1709 Economic depression; many slaves were brought to the domestic market for sale

1713 The first smallpox epidemic at the Cape decimated the Khoi, scared away the survivors, and led to a sharp labour shortage

1717 VOC decided to end assisted European family immigration to the Cape on the grounds that the free wage labour experiment had failed. The Company decided to retain slavery as the principal source of labour for the Cape

1725 Reports of runaway slaves living at Hangklip (across modern False Bay); their colony continued to exist until the nineteenth century

1739-48 Spain imposes severe losses on all types of sea-borne traffic, thus setting off a long depression in the Cape

1755 Smallpox epidemic with heavy losses among Cape Lodge slaves

1767 Importing male slaves from Asia prohibited; another outbreak of smallpox in the Lodge

1770 Comprehensive revision of the Statutes of India, leading to possible manumission of slaves under certain conditions, and emancipation of the so-called 'courtesan slaves' (female slaves permitted to live with European male visitors who paid an agreed amount to the owners)

1771 About 100 slaves from Bengal landed at the Cape

1777 Ruling that once a slave is baptised, he or she cannot be sold

1779 'Patriot uprising' of Cape settlers when they sent a petition directly to VOC authorities in Holland for permission to mete out punishment to their slaves themselves

1780 Collapse of Dutch transoceanic shipping

1780-84 Anglo-Dutch War inflicted heavy losses on Dutch shipping. The decline of the Dutch East India Company

1793 Tuan Guru's release from prison; this is regarded as a key event in the consolidation of the Islamic community of the Cape

1795 The British occupation of the Cape during the Napoleonic wars. The British remained in control throughout the nineteenth century, except for a short period of Dutch rule during 1803-06. The demise of the Dutch East India Company

1796 The British administration banned torture of slaves and some of the cruelest forms of capital punishment

1802 End of British administration of the Cape; Dutch rule (new name, Batavian Republic) re-established

1803-06 Revolutionary Batavian government in the Cape

1807 Britain passed law (Slave Trade Abolition Act) banning slave trade in British territories; slavery was still legal

1808 Slave Trade Abolition Act enforced; suppression of the oceanic slave trade

1808 Koeberg slave uprising, led by Louis of Mauritius and Abraham van der Kaap, was crushed

1811 Another outbreak of smallpox in the Lodge

1812 Repeal of a clause of the Statutes of India that pronounced that baptised slaves should enjoy freedom like other Christians

1816 Assisted European family immigration to the Cape was allowed once again

1820 Ordinance 20 abolished serfdom and thus liberated the Khoi from many restrictions imposed on them

1822 The last recorded import of slaves by illegal means. Slaves were allowed to marry legally

1823 The Nineteenth Ordinance extended legal sanction to slave marriages

1825 A slave uprising led by Galant van der Kaab in the Koue Bokkeveld (now Cedarberg, near Ceres) was suppressed

1826 Appointment of an official protector (guardian) of slaves with lower level assistant protectors in settlements away from Cape Town. Fresh permission for assisted European family immigration to the Cape was withdrawn

1828 Ordinance 50 (labelled locally as the law for the emancipation of Hottentots) served to redress some of the wrongs hitherto perpetrated against Khoi peoples, thus virtually liberating them from serfdom

1830 Cape administration ordered slave owners to maintain records of punishments meted out to their slaves

1831 Slave owners in Stellenbosch opposed keeping records of punishments to which slaves were subjected

1833 The Orphan Chamber stopped functioning

1834 Abolition of slavery throughout the British Empire

1834 Introduction of the apprenticeship system for emancipated slaves under which 'freed' slaves were required to work for their owners for another four years after freedom as 'apprentices' without any pay so that they could be 'fit for freedom'

1838 End of the four-year apprenticeship system

1838 Emancipation of slaves effected; slaves were freed on Emancipation Day, 1 December

1841 Promulgation of the Masters and Servants Ordinance that was in force until 1974; this law made desertion, negligence in duty, insubordination, and use of insulting language criminal offences

1856 The Masters and Servants Ordinance was given additional teeth

1910 Katie Jacobs, the ninety-six-year-old last Creole slave, was interviewed by a journalist for her reminiscences. The text of the interview was published in *African People's Organization Newsletter*

1974 The Masters and Servants Ordinance was repealed

Appendix B

Glossary

Apprentice
A former slave who was forced to work for his or her former owner without pay. In terms of legislation, freed slaves had to be apprenticed to their former masters for four years between 1834 and 1838

Bandiet or Banditi
Convict

Burgher
A free white citizen of the Cape colony. In 1655, the VOC gave permission to a small number of officials to become free burghers in order to cultivate wheat near the fort. Two years later in February 1657, the first nine free burghers were each given a farm along the border of the Colony. In 1662, the number of free burghers rose to sixty, most of whom were wheat farmers. Large-scale immigration of Europeans started from the Netherlands and neighbouring countries towards the close of the seventeenth century

Bywoners
Whites who squatted on land belonging to burghers

Caffers
Members of the police force forming the executive branch of the Fiscal. Originally, the term was applied to African slaves, mostly from Angola. Later, there are references to Asian full-breed Caffers

Commandos
Armed groups of burghers on horseback who chased runaway slaves

Creole
Slaves born in the Cape

Droster
An escaped slave

Fiscal
Number two (accord to some, the third-in-command) in the hierarchy of company officials who was charged with slaves' welfare before 1828

Free blacks	Persons of African and Asian origin who were not slaves. Freed or manumitted slaves also became free blacks
Halfslag	People with some European blood; half-caste or half-breed slaves
Heelslag	Indigenous people undiluted by European blood
Knecht	An overseer of slaves given to burghers on loan by the Company, a knecht, usually a male white, was given full control over slaves in an outpost or the main farm, especially in the absence of the master. However, knechts also performed other jobs, including teaching. Apart from Company knechts, there were free knechts who worked without a contract, after negotiating their own terms and conditions of service
Landdrost	Local magistrate
Mandoor or Mandador	Portuguese name for a slave overseer in charge of other slaves
Manumission	Freeing of slaves by owners
MOOC	Master of the Orphan Chamber
Mulatto	Slaves, sometimes called halfslag (or half-breed), who were the offspring of a European father and a non-European mother
Opgaaf	Documents of census of the Colony
Orphan Chamber	Set up in the seventeenth century to look after and safeguard the interests of orphaned children
Peculium	A slave's salary, usually paid in kind at the Cape
Placcaat	A statute displayed on a poster for general notification regarding a new regulation or administrative order

Plagium	The practice of kidnapping persons of African and Asian origin leading to their enslavement
'Prize Negroes'	Illegal black slaves who were captured and seized by the British on French or Portuguese vessels after the abolition of the slave trade (by the British) and were brought to the Cape. They were mainly from Mozambique and Madagascar. 'Prize' Negroes were obliged to serve their masters for fourteen years without wage. At the end of this period, they were 'free'. Ironically, this freedom made little sense to them as it was attended by no concerted efforts at rehabilitation. It is estimated that at least 2,000 'Prize Negroes' were brought to the Cape Colony in the decade after the British ban on the slave trade in 1807 (Worden et al., 1996: 92). Prize Negroes and their descendants were eventually absorbed into the emerging 'Coloured' community of the Cape and were targets of Islamic proselytisation
Rixdaalder (**Rixdollar**)	Unit of currency
Sjambok	Heavy four-foot-long whip made of solid rhinoceros or hippopotamus hide for flogging used on slaves and for driving cattle
VOC	Verenigde Oostindische Compagnie (Dutch East India Company). The VOC administered the Cape Colony from 1652 to 1795 and was replaced by the British
Werf	Area around the main house often surrounded by a boundary wall or outbuildings
Wetnurse	A black woman whose job it was to breastfeed her employer's baby

Appendix C

Inventory of Bengali Slaves in the Cape
(Arranged in alphabetical order)

Name	Age at 1st Ref	Owner(s)	From	After freedom Important Events
Aaron	1726			
Aaron	17 1699	Joris Brunt	Jan v. Meerland	
Aaron vBeng	1717 about 40 years	Death for attempted arson of master Pieter v de Westhuijsen's winestore		
Aaron	1722	Vonnis		
Aaron vBeng	1726	Worked on cattlepost of mistress Ten Damme	Was a ringleader of a group of runaway slaves—was never convicted; seemingly avoided capture	
Abdula	1823	Lady Campbell requests permission to return Abdula, a free black , to Bengal		
Abraham	27/28 1677			
Abraham	30 1689	Gerhard Coutier	Johannes Blesius	
Abraham	18 1689	Thomas March	Cornelia S. Botma	
Abraham				
Abraham VS	1752	Married Lena vdk VS		
Abraham	1756	Vossis		
Abraham	1760s?	Married? Rosetta v. Bengale VS/ kind =Rachel 1768		
Abraham	1845	a Coolie	Death notice	
Achillis	1807	Will +will of wife, Sounting v. Bougies		
Achillis	1835	Will+will of wife, Sounting v. Bougies		
Adam	23/24 1698	Jan Direx de Beer	Hendrik Cornelis Olivier	
Adam vBeng	1791 30yrs	Bondsman of Johs. Hendrik Roux/ thrashed by Petrus Joubert, son of another burgher/ Roux complained to landdrost/ seems no action taken		
Adam	1820	'Lyfeigen van Arend de Waal'/Vonnis		

Achmet/
Achmat

Adolph	1801	Joachim Itzen transferred slave to David Benjamin Kuuhl	
Adonis	1796	Freed by Gerrit Gertsen	
Alexander	15 1697	Henrik Stirk	Johannes Pithius
Alexander	1699	Vonnis	

Death on: Sunday 27.05.1731 Alexander, male,
not mentioned, seasoned, unknown, **description
in original** N : *volwasse* slaaf,

Alexander	1732	Vonnis	
Alexander	1737	Vonnis	
Alina	4/9/1669	Sold by Goens (jr) Rijcklof v. at 70	To Coon Johannes at 7 0 Bought by To Vauwenburg
	5/28/1669	Sold by Coon Johannes at 80	
Amarentia	1762	Testament	
Amerentia	1754	Testament	
Amerentia	1762	Will +wife of Augustyn of Bengalen	
Amerentia	1795	Soldier Jacob Frederik Reinhaut transferred her to Michiel Stigling	
Amie/F?	1791	Gideon Rossouw	Buys (or sells?) her
Andebo (Swartland)	1763	Married ? Anna, Hottentotin/ k= Diana 1763	
Andries	1695	Attina Pieck	Albert Coopman
Andries	27 1697	Ditlof Croes	Hendrik Sneewint
Andries	20 1697	Johannes Clijn	Christiaen Elers
Andries	1697	Vonnis?	
Andries vBeng	1741 Tried for suicide	Johannes Louw Jacobsz	
Andries	1760	Vonnis	
Andries VS (Cf Magdalena v Bengalen	1762	Married Magdalena v. Bengale VS	

Andries	1770	Testament	
Andries vCalkuta	1786; 25 years/ probably obtained from British traders in Calc.	Runaway slave of dragoon, Christiaan Velbron; executed	
Angela		Daughter, Maria Basson, married Christian Maasdorp	
Angela OR Angila', 'Ansielaar', 'Ansiela', 'Ansla', and 'Hansela	1706	Kontrakte/ widow of Arnoldus Willemsz Basson	
Ansla	1720	Liquidation & Distribution Account	
Anna	1669		
Anna	22/23 1692	C.J.Simons	Hendrik Cornelis
Anna	22 1698	Cornelis Keeleman	Gerrit Meyer
Anna Grootheyning	1713	Married Christiaan Bok	
Anna Groothenning		Daughters Maria Bock v de Caap + Anna Bock	Christo van Rensburg <montxsuz.cs>
Anna Groothenning		Extramarital with Jacob Marik/ K=Jacob 1718	
Anna Groothenning		Had extramarital Rel with her master Hans Casper Geringer	
Anna		Daughter=Catharina Bok married Jacob Etienne Gous in 1718	
Anna	1724	Her daughter, Anna Bok, married Andries Bester	
Anna	1785	Vonnis	
Anna Rebecca	1722	Testament	
Anna Rebecca	1724	Testament	
Anna Rebecca	1731	Married Arnoluds Koevoet (Coevoet)	
Anna Rebecca	1731	Will	
Anna Rebecca	1731	Testament	
Anna de Koning	1678	Married Oloff Bergh	
Annica vBeng	1667? Wife of Anthony v.Japan		

Anthoni Anthonij	1721	Vonnis		
Anthonij	1678			
Anthonij (late free burgher)	1683	Slave Pouwlus sold to Oeloff Bergh by Orphan Masters from estate of deceased Anthonij, the late free burgher		
Anthonijsz v Beng	1755?	Mentioned as free black Anthonij v Beng @ Opgaaf rolle		
Anthonij	24/25 1695	Jonal Marsman	Jam Fuber	
Anthonij	45 1697	Marten v.d.Vijver	Cornelis Botma	
Anthonij	20 1699	Joris Brunt	Samuel Elsevier	
Anthonij	18 1699	Joan v. Hoorn	Gifted to Joan v. Rotterdam	Condition=JvRott not to sell slave + he should be freed on death
Anthonij	1730	Vonnis		
Anthonij	1745	Vonnis		
Anthonij	1767	Vonnis		
Anthonij vBeng	1786	Vonnis; runaway bondsman of burgher fire-master, Arend v Wielig	Sentenced	
Anthonij Jansz v Beng	1682	Purchased by Basson		
Anthony	1767	Swapped for Rosetta		
Anthony	26 1697	Jacobus Hercht	Henning Husing	
Anthony	24 1697	Johan Lispensier	Free Black Mira Moor	
Anthony	1754	Testament		
Antje/F	1796	Hermanus Babier Carel Smit		
	1797	Same as above		
Antony	10/1673			
Antonij v Beng	1690	His son=Christoffel Snyman married Marguerite de Savoye in 1690		
Antony	1690s-1703	Married? Maria van Batavia		
Antony VS	1751	Married Wilhelmina v. Maccasar		

Antonika	24 1697		
Antonika	24 1697	Jan Buys	Anna Hendrina v. Otteren
Antoniko /F	24 1699	Hendrina v. Otteren (widow of Hendrik Barent Oldenland)	Jacob v. Paassen
Apollos	1795	Joseph Virony transferred him to Jan de Vos	
Apollos	1815	'Lyfeigen van Gerrit Scholtz'/ Vonnis	
Appollos	1809	Vonns	
April	1732	Vonnis	
April	1762	Vonnis	
April	1780	Vonnis	
April	1788	Vonnis	
April	1796	Pieter Henkes transferred him to Carel Christiaan Schmidt	
April	1797	Johannes Grosch transferred slave to Pieter Cilliers	
April	1800	Freed by Frederik Louis	
April	1833	Application for deed of burghership	
Arend	22 1700	Olof Bergh	To mother-in-law, Angela Bassoon
Arie vBeng	'Not found in the Company books'		
Aron	20 1695	Michiel de Keyser	Hendrik Barent Oldenland
Aron	20 1698	Andries de Looper	Hans Jurgen Grimpe
Aron	1697	Vonnis	
Aron	10/6/1744 Death	Bandiet en Jongen	
Aron	17/1/1747 Death	Bandiet en Jongen	
August	1796	Fredrik Leubegoud transferred him to Frederik Bielefeld	
August	1806	Applied to free slave Theresia	
August	1810	Owner, Regina's appl. To emancipate him	
Augustijn	12 1697	Bartholomeus v.d. Velde	Abraham Hartog
Augustijn	20/21 1690	Jan de Marre	Jan Wessels

Augustijn	22 1697	Jan Buys	Cornelis Victor
Augustyn	1686	Married Sara van Ceylon	
Augustyn (cf 3 rows below)	1762	Will + will of wife Amerentia	
Augustus	13/14 1698	Leendert van Deendert v.Deijl	Simon v.d.Stel
Augustus	14 September 1720	Slave of Angela vBeng/ auctioned on farm Hondswijk after Angela's death	
Augustus	1720	Vonnis	
Augustinus VS	1741	Married Emmerentia/Esperance of Bengal VS	
Aurora	1799	Johannes Ley	Abraham d.Smit
Baksoe	1822	Will + will of wife, Maria van Bengalen (2CNA243/267)	
Baltsen	1717	Slave of Westhuijsen—See Aaron	
Barent	16 1699	Adriaan v.d. Stel	To brother, Jonker Frans v.d. Stel
Bastiaan	20 1697	Jan Buys	Jan Hendrik Voogt
Bastiaen	25 1685	Steward of Nieuwlandt	
Bastiana	1720	Testament +wife of Abraham van Madagascar'swill	
Batua	1797	Vonnis	
Bazette	1798	Power of attorney given to him	By Oloff Godlieb de Wet
Betty	8 1698	William Erle	Jan Brommert
Bietja (freed slave woman)	1800	Contract bet. Her & Frederik Lelie re: slave Apeil of Simauba	
Bijgeval	24/25 1694	Jan Stam	Henning Husing
Bluskam	22/23 1691	Gualtor Goddard	Catharina Theunisz
Boer	17/18 1692	S. de Jonge	Adriaan van Brakel
Camonie	1798	Christian Bossert C. Bossert	Frederik Reinhoud
(Carmonie)	1798		Hendrik v.d.Graaf

Canai		Freed by Johannes Gysbertus Blanckenberg &Hendrik v.d. Graaf, Executor of estate of late JJ Breyer	
Canai (Kanai)	1806	Application to free slave, Anisa	
Candace Cf.Fortuyn	1799	Andries Muller transferred him +1 to Carel Scheiffel of Robben Island	
Canterbury	1798	Freed by Dorothea E. Schiller	
Canterburry (free black)	1802	Security bond given by Hermanus Keeve & Petrus Johannes Keeve	
Cardace	1802	Freed by Barend van Blerk, executor of estate of late Johannes Keyzer	
Carel	23/24 1692	Jan Hanegrif	Guillam Heems
Carel	1726	Hendriksz Van Rheenen	Owner gifted his estate to Carel
Carel	1728	Vonnis	
Carel Jansz	1734	Testament	
Carel Jansz	1737	Testament	
Carel Jansz	1744	Liquidation & Distribution Account	
Carel Lodewyk Blume	1798	Not a slave?	
Carnap	1799	Freed by Dirk Gysbert v.Reenen	
Casar	1840	apprentice	Death notice
Catharina	Late 1600s		
Catharina	1682	Married Harmen Bartolomena/ k=Maurits Jacobs 1682	
Catharina	1702	Married Maurits Jacobs/ k=Maurits Jacobs 1682 Daughter, Anna	
Catharina		Her daughter, Maria Boomgaard married Andre Friedrich Chritoffel in 1797	
Catharina v. Bengale	1671	Married to De Later VS Japan	
Catharina Opklim VS	1694	Husband = JW Vermeulen (Utrecht)	Same as Catrijn v. Bengale
Catharina (free settler) Catharina Vrijman?	1702 (same as above)	Mentioned in a List of Cape District +husband, Jan Willemsz Vermeulen + 5 children	

Catharina (free settler)	1702 (same as above)	Wife of Andries Vermeulen mentioned in Muster roll of Stellenbosch/ 1694 they married after slave bore him 4 children Ref. Muster roll Stellenbosch, 1702
Catharina Catharina VS	(same as above)	Daughter, Anna Vermeulen, married Jean Durand in 1702 Daughter 2, Maria Vermeulen, married Johannes Rogier in 1705
Catharina Anthonis	1656	Born in Zalegon, Beng. Brought to Cape1656. Freed 1656 sans compensation so that she could be married to Jan Woutersz. Resolution of 26/4/56 called 'de eerbare Jongedochter Cath Anth.'
Catrijn Catryn?	26/1677	Slave of Cornelis Classen who had 3(?) children by her who were all baptized/contemporary records. Catryn='gedoopte swartinne'
Cecilia	1706	W.W.van der Stel Baptized 1706
Cecilia	1720s	Cecilia's daughter, Helen Valentyn, married son of Raja ofTambora who converted to Christianity
Cecilia	1716	Married Hecules Valentyn vd Kus
Cecilia (Sibella?)	1730s?	Married Hercules Valentyn
Catrina	1713	Testament
Cesar	1809	Master, Jan van Bougies applied to free Cesar
Cezar /M	8 1695	Thomas Evans for
	8/8 1695	Joan de Klerck Jan Feuber
Christian		Daughter, Johanna Catharina Markse, married Louis Picard of Amsterdam in 1746
Christijn	1678	
Christina VS	1735	Married Frans Hendrik Mark (Duitsland)
Christina	1741	Married Hendrik Frans(e)
Christina	1787	Daughter, Helena Alida Picard, married Abraham Ventura 1787
Christina Casta	1677	
Cipido	1800	Daniel de Waal transferred slave to Johan Ulrich Kiebourg
Claas	20/1674	
Claas		
Claas		

Claas	1675	Vonnis	
Claas	11/12 1676		
Claas	1677		
Claas	1679		
Claas	27/28 1692	Egbert Kalf	Henning Husing
Claas		Married? Cecilia van Macassar/ k=Flora 1695	
Claas	1692	Albert Coopman	1692 Conditonal Manumission Sold back to Hendrik Bouman for f400 Should work for 2 yrs. Deed cancelled on 29/4/93 as he 'behaved badly'
	1694		
	1695	Boeseken161 Boeseken164 Boeseken171	freed by Bouman on payment of f500
Claas	1692 25 1695	Andries de Mann As above (for Agate Cornelia Six	Hendrik Bouman Pierre Simond
Claas	19 1698	Johannes v.Rennen	Hendrik Bouman
Claas	17/18 1693	Jacob van Amerongen	Jan Mrijndertsz Cruywagen
Claas VS	1695	Married? Jannetje Gerrits	
Claas	28 1696	Frans v.d.Stael	Carel Carelse
Claas	20 1697	Coenraad Warner	Jan Wessels
Claas (dateDeath	14/2/1742 Death *Kloeke jongen*		
Claas vBeng	1744	Anna Marais	Fought with another slave over favours of Aurora, slavinne; punishment whipped & sent back to mistress
Claas & Anna	1665		
Claas Claasz (free settler)	1702	Mentioned in a List of Cape District	

Claas Gerritz v Bengale			
Claes			
Claes	12/13 1677		
Claes v. Bengale	27/28 1677		
Claes	1682 1683	Jacob Aersse Brouwer	
Claes	28 1695	Borchart Brant	Freed before Return to Europe
Claes Kath	1682	Hester van Lier	
Clara vdk/ Bengale?		Married? Philippus vdk/ k=Juliana P. 1712	
Clara	1722	Extramarital relation with Paulus Brons/ Child, Anna, born in 1722	
Clasina	6/1742 1811		
Cleleli	1739	Daughter=Eva vdk VS married Pieter Lange	
Colvins (of Calcutta)	1798	Not slave?	
Cornelis	30 1695	Jan Vlasblom	Simon van der Stael
Coridon	17 1695	Claes Bronckhorst	Joris v. Straalen + Jacob Doornik
Coridon	13 1697	Abraham de Hartog	Albert Barent Gildenhuys
Coridon	24 1698	Frederick Meyer	Andries Pietersz
Coridon Bengal or Ceylon	?-1797		
Coridon	1794 1807		
Constantia		Married? Arend of Maccasar/ kind=Johanna 1712	
Constantia	1727	Testament	
Constantia	1727	Will	
Corydon	1742		

Csebruarij (Februarij?) healthy, seasoned, unknown,	death on: on Thursday 13.09.1759 *kloeke jongen*, C 2542 133			
Cupido	1681	Vonnis (2CNA140/267)		
Cupido	10 1672			
Cupido	1676			
Cupido	24/25 1694	Jan Stam	Henning Husing	
Cupido	20 1697	Jan Nobel	Jacob Vogel	
Cupido	1727	Vonnis		
Cupido	1732	Vonnis		
Cupido vBemg	1745; *jongen*; died before conviction			Murdered a *meijd* Francina
Cupido	4/6/1747Death Bandiet en Jongen			
Cupido	1760	Vonnis		
Cupido male, healthy, seasoned, N : *kloeke jongen*, C 2598 78	death on: on Tuesday 18.10.1774			
Dam	1756	Vonnis		
Dam	1779	Vonnis		
Dam, male, slave healthy, seasoned, unknown, N : *kloeke jongen*, C 2593 105	death on: Thursday 30.09.1773			

Dama male, healthy, seasoned, dispens, *kloeke jongen* van't *gemene werk*, C 2650 99	Date of death on: on Sunday 28.12.1788		
Daman	1767-68		
Damon	1764		
Damon	1812	'Lyfeigen van de vrijzwart Abdul Rajab'/ Vonnis	
Daniel	25 1700	Rijckus v. Kerlik for Cornelis Chastelyn	Henning Husing
Daniel	1819	Will+Will of wife, Flora van Bengalen	
Darius	20 1697	Arnoldus Muykens	Hendrik Smit
David	1728	Vonnis	
David vBeng	1750	Jan Lodenwijk Bouwer	Accused his master had beaten the slave Alexander vMallebaar causing death/ Master not convicted for insufficient evidence/ David whipped for making false accusation & returned to his owner
David	1799	Freed by Jacob Laubscher	
David	1817	Seeking permission to Manumit a slave	
David	1827	Will	
David	1835	Death notice	
De Later, Antony (Japan)	1666+1673	Marriage 1 with Annika van Bengale 1666 + 2 with Lijsbet van Bengale 1673	
De Later, Antony VS (Japan)	1671 Same as above	Married Catharina v. Bengale VS	
Delphina	1756	Testament	
Delphina	1764	Testament	
Diana	1666		
Diana v Beng	1728		
Diana	1756	Vonnis	

Diana	1795	Jacobus Pieter Hugo transferred her to sailor David Leenhardt	
Diana +5 children	1797	Daniel Frederik Immelman sold to Anna Heyning	
Diana	1797	Johan Heinrich Richter transferred her to Pieter Henkes	
Diana	1828	Will	
Diana	1835	Death notice	
Doevert	17 1698	Jan Direx de Beer	Hendrik Cornelis Olivier
Dominga + Domingo from Bengal +1 Sl. From Macassarc	25/26 1686	Simon v.d. Stel	Matthijs Greve
Domingo v Beng	1655	Van Riebeeck bought him + Angela from Commander Pieter Kemp	
Domingo v. Bengale	1659	Name mentioned in a a doc. dealing with Khoikhoi issue	
Domingo/M	1681		
Domingo	1691	Married Maria van Bengale	
Domingo	1686		
Domingo	32/33 1692	Pieter Hermans	Lambert Adriaens
Domingo	20 1694	William Madowal	No buyer mentioned
Domingo (free settler in Cape District)	1702	Mentioned in a list + wife, Maria v. Bengalen	
Domingo	1712	Will	
Domingo v. Bengale	1726	Mentioned in doc. With Pieter Cruijsser as master; nothing else known	
Domingo	1726	Vonnis	
Domingo	1737		
Domingo aka Jieman Pavian	Death 11/8/1744		
Jieman Pavian	*Bandiet en Jongen*		
Domingo	1781	Vonnis	
Domingo	1798	Gerrit v.Wyk transferred him to Georg Ulrich Moll	

Domingo	1799	Johan Abraham Moes transferred slave to Johannes Heyne	
Domingo	1816	'Lyfeigen van de weduwe M Hertzog'/ Vonnis	
Domingo	1830	Will+ will of Stantie v.d.Kaap-wife	
Dorothea /F	20 1699	Jan Direx de Beer for Margareta Swanenburg	Jacob Krebs
	20 1699	Jacob Krebsz	Jan Willem Vermeulen of Utreecht
Dorothea VS (Vryswart)	1772&1780	Was freed 1772/ married Ahlers, Oltman	
Dorothea		Daughter, Rachel Ahlers, married Gehardus Hermanus Onken in c. 1790	
Dorothea (widow of Oltman Ahlers)	1791	Married Johan Thomas Petrus Petersen	
Dorothea		Daughter, Rachel Ahlers, married Friedrich Monk	
Dorothea	1792	Will; wife of Johan Thomas Pietersen	
Dorothea (widow of Thomas Pieterse(n))	1795	Gave power of attorney to	To Jacob Hendriksen
	1795 1796	Obligation to Fire Master	
Eizabeth Rebecca VS	1755	Married Andries Meyer (Danzig)	
Emaniul	1680	Vonnis	
Engela	1718	Testament	
Esperance	1739	Testament	
Eva	1762	Testament	
Eva VS	1756	Barend v. Batavia's 2 marriage with Eva	
Eva	1762 As above	Will; Wife of Barend v. Batavia	
Faquir	1806	Vonnis	
Februarij	1773	Testament	
Februarij	1773	Will; Filed in 1782	
Februarij	1781	Vonnis	
Februarij	1784	Vonnis	

Februarij	1797	Vonnis		
February	1810	Will+ will of Roosie v.v.Kaap		
February	1810	Applied to free his slave, Mina of the Cape		
February+3	1811	Request for fining them for not having a retail licence, remitted		
February	1838	Death notice		
Flora		Married? Hanibal van Kus /k=Johanna 1718		
Flora	1728	Testament		
Flora	1728	Wife of Carel Jansz's will		
Flora	1734	Will		
Flora	1737	Testament		
Flora VS	1764	Married Christiaan Johannes vd Kus VS		
Flora	1796	Rosa Catharina Pittscher transferred her to Frederik Gebhard		
Flora	1799	Being posted as security by Johanna de Necker		
				Johannes
	1799	JJF Wagener		Bleuser
	1799	Johanna de Necker		Constant v.Nuldt Onkruydt
Flora	1799	Notarial protocol-Deed of Transfer by Johannes Blesser to Johannes Petrus Stagman		
Flora	1834	Will (Flora=wife of Soesong vd Kaap		
Floris M	24 1695			
Flora	1834	Death notice		
Floris M	24 1695	Christiaan Martens	Mahu de Rijcke	
			Joost Cornelis	
	25 1700	Mahu de Rijcke		
Floris, Susanna Meynert	1765	Testament		
Floris M	1801	Andries Staphanus du Toit transferred slave to Gerrit Jacobus Koekemoer		
Floor	20 1690	Abrahm Post	Cornelis Pietersz LInnes	

Fortuin	1799	Andreas de Roos transferred him to Johannes H. Neethling	
Fortuin	1806	His master, Maria, applied to free him	
Fortuin (free black)	1811	Applied to free his slave girl, Sara	
Fortuijn vBeng	1739	Abraham Decker	Gave testimony in trial of Alexander vMaccaser
Fortuijn	1737	Vonnis	
Fortuijn vBeng	1742; 28 years; burnt alive	Abraham de Villers= master; Attempted burning of farm of Pieter Venter where lived his consort, Christijn v de Caab	
Fortuijn	1742	Vonnis	
Fortuijn	1745	Vonnis	
Fortuijn	1750	Vonnis	
Fortuijn de 1 de de eerste, male, seasoned, unskilled, unknown,	death Thursday 20.12.1753 **On**bequaame jongen, C 2524 93		
Fortuijn	1780	Vonnis	
Fortuijn	1781	Vonnis	
Fortuijn, male, bandiet, seasoned, dispens,: bandiet en jong uijt de dispens van de oude slaven, C 2638 20	Date of death on: on Saturday 27.05.1786 bandiet en jongen oude slave, C 2638 27		
Fortuin, male, healthy, seasoned, N : kloeke jongen, C 2628 66	Date of death on: on Wednesday 23.10.1782		

Fortuin (Swartland) Bengale		Married? Elizabeth Hottentottin / k=David 1763
Fortuyn	1797	Michiel Kieswetter transferred him to Francois Le Clus
Fortuyn	1797	Pieter Francois Le Clus transferred slave to Frans La Boscagne
Fortuyn (Cf. Candace)	1799	Andries Muller transferred him to Carel Scheiffel of Robben Island
Fortuyn	1801	Wilhelmina v.d.Poel, widow of Jacob Swanevelder, transferred slave to Hendrik Cloete
Fortuyn	1811	Requested release of a slave woman, Eva
Francies	1797	Commissioner of Civil & Marriage Affairs, Daniel de Waal transferred slave to Adriaan Myndert van Schoor
Francina		
Francina	1677	
Francis	22/23 1693	Jan de With Christiaen Fraser
Francois	20 1700	Theunis Direx v. Harman Schalkwijck Barentsz
Francois	1800	Thomas Lindley transferred slave to Bartholomeus Durham
Frans	1807	Applied to free slave Lindor
Frans	1797	Cornelis Gysbert Verwey transferred slave to Arend v. Wielligh
Frans	1798	Bond of security given for him by Jan Pieter Baumgardt & Egbertus Bletterman
Frans	Around1800	Led Moslem delegation to Sir George Young to request site for a mosque
Frans	1801	Jan Daniel Alders transferred slave to Hendrik Nieuwkerk
Frans (freed slave)	1799	Deed of Mortgage given for him by Jan Pieter Baumgardt & Frederik Bielefeld
Frans	20 1700	Pieter v.Convent Jacobus de Wit
Gedull, male, healthy, seasoned, : *kloeke jongen*, C 2623 84	Date of death on: on Monday 22.01.1781	
Gedult	1795	Freed by Jan Pieter Faure

Gerhard Ewoud Overbeek	1797	Mentioned in the will of JJF Wagener	
Gerrit	1676		
Geertruy Helena	1785	Married Jacob of Ceylon VS/ Jacob =ex-slave	
Geertruijda	1805	Will; Wife of Jacob van Ceijlon	
Gertruyda Helena	1785	Testament	
Gertruyda Helena	1790	Testament	
Goliath	1761	Vonnis	
Gusdtinho	30 1695	Reijner de Vos	Matthijs Greeff
Hameling, Pieter a.k. Pieter v Bengale (VS)	1734	Married Johanna Arends vdk =VS	
Hanne	1800	Andries Dirkse transferred her to Johannes Jacobus Vos	
Hannibal	25 1687		
Hannibal	20 1689	Dominique De Chavonnes	Henning Husing
Hannibal	15/16 1692	Gerrit Rouquendorp	Eric Jansz Hillebrand
Hannibal	21/22 1694	Andries de Man	Pieter van der Bijl
Hannibal	1695	Andries de Mann For Joan v.Hoorn	Matthijs Greeff
Hannibal	32 1695	Claes Bronckhorst	Henning Husing
Hannibal	28 1697	Abraham Boon	Frederick Russouw de Wit
Hannibal	1813	'Lyfeigen van EF Schrader'/ Vonnis	
Hans	1743	Francina Bevernagie	VOC asked to take over
Hans	20/21 1695	Jacob Landsheer	Jan Dircx de Beer

Harip, male, healthy, seasoned, unknown, N: *kloeke jongen*, C 2588 118	death on Wednesday 24.06.1772	
Harmen Bartolomeus	1682	Married Catharina v. Bengale/ k=Maurits Jacobs 1682
Harroe, male, slave healthy, seasoned,: *kloeke jongen*, C 2599 98	death on: Sunday 15.01.1775	
Hect	1829	Memo recd. Re: remission of fine
Hector Casta	1678	
Helena v. Bengale	1739	Extramarital relations with Cornelis de Vries Daughter= Cornelia Helena
Helena vBengale (As above)		Daughter, Juliana Moses (Jacobse), married Friedrich August Hertzog in 1760
Helena van *Persien*	1775	Widow of Pieter van Bengalen Testament + Will
Hendrica Johanna		Extramarital Jacobus Matthiam Kluysman
Hendrik VS	1773	Married Sara Elizabeth vdk
Hendriks Adriaan VS	1771	Married Sara vdk
Hendriks, Johannes	1774	Testament
Hercuur	1781	Vonnis
Imam Achmat	Around1825 1740-1843	
Immamedie	1781	Vonnis
Isaak	1668	
Isaac	1701	Married Maria vd Kus
Isaac (free settler)	1702	Name in a list +wife, Maria v Coromandel
Isaacs AlbertVS	1761	Married her exMistress, Helena Johanna v. Ceylon

Isaakse, Albert	1771	Testament		
Isak	21 1672			
Isak	25 1697	Hendrik v. Buyenhem	Theunis Direx v. Schalkwijck	
Isak	1710	Liquidation & Distribution account		
Isak vBeng	1668 Slave of Z. Wagenaer			Kinders174
Isak vBeng	1714			CAD C336, SLodge Census1714/Shell, *Lodge Roots*, Entry 176, p32
Isak Casta	1677			
Isabel + 2sons (3yrs & 6 months)	17/18 1693	Hendrijk Persijn	Gerrit Jannsz van Deventer	
Izaak	23 1697	Johannes Ckein for Jan Willaris		
Jacob/M	1680			
Jacob	28 1697	Bartholomeus v.d. Velde	Francois v.d. Stel	
Jacob vBeng	1738	Bondsman of widow Steven Viret; Along with 2 free blacks +3slavesfound in streets after 10pm Were whipped & sent home to work in chains		
Jacobs, Salomon	18Century	Freed slave married a white woman, Anna Elizabeth Zeeman / See under Salomon		
Jacques	18/19 1692	Will Deeron	Guilliam Heems	
Jacob	12 1699	Coenradus Cock	Jan Brommert	Condition= Cock be allowed to buy back slave should he return
Jacob	1741	Vonnis		
Jacob assumed in Lodge, male, slave healthy, seasoned, unknown,	death Wednesday 03.05.1752			
Jan	1745	Vonnis		

Jan	20/1674		
Jan	1678		
Jan /M	24 15.3.1695		
Jan	24 1695	Remeus Oole	Simon v.v. Stael
	14.9.1695	Simon v.d. Stael	Henning Husing
Jan/ M	1666		
Jan: *male,: bandiet en jongen,* C 2572 71	Death on Friday 20.05.1768		
Jan vBeng	1786	Vonnis; runaway bondsman of burgher fire-master, Arend v Wielig	Punished but not executed
Jan Horl	14/15 1692	Bernt Borchard	Jan de Souza
Jan van Oldenburgh	1680		
Janna/F	12/	Hertzog	
Janna/F / Same as above?			
Jansen Jan	1762	Married Clara v. Batavia	
Jansen Hendrik VS	1773	Married Sylvia Maria v. Madagascar	
Jansz, Carel	1728	Testament	
Jansz, Carel	1741	Testament	
Jansz, Hendrik	1778	Testament	
Jansz, Johannes	1720	Testament	
Jansz, Johannes	1747	Testament	
Jansz, Willem	1773	Testament	

Janze, Willem	1789	Testament		
Jantje	11 1665			
Jantje	13 1699	Jacob van Hoorn	Adriaan Cortman	Gifted to Cortman; owner leaving; on condition that Cortman does not sell J and that he will stipulate in his will that J to be freed on his death
Jan Willemsz Vermeulen	1702	Name in List of Cape District +wife, Catharina v. Bengalen		
Januarij	1736	Vonnis		
Januarij	1737	Vonnis		
Januarij	1742	Vonnis		
Januarij	1744 (in Robben)/ was *bandiet* later appointed a *caffer*			
Januarij	1760	Vonnis		
Januarij	1762	Vonnis		
Januarij	1767	Vonnis		
Januarij	1772	Vonnis		
Januarij	1778	Vonnis		
Januarij	1797	Vonnis		
Januarij	1820	Will		
Januarij	1820	Will		
Januarij	1833	Will		
January	1790	Daniel Petrus Haupt to purchase J from Captain Kudde		
January	1797	Stabbed another slave due to sexual jealousy		
January	1800	Jacob Frederik Reynhout transferred him to Hermanus Koen		
January	1800	Notarial protocol re: special power of attorney February to January		
January of Bengalen and a young slave, Titus, also of Bengalen, were cripples. Their worth was Rd:s20 and Rd:s15 respectively. Both these slaves belonged to Baltus Roelofsz				
January	1801	Vonnis		

January	1808	His master applied to free him
January(free black)	1829	Exemption from payment of taxes
Jasfoe male, healthy, seasoned, unknown, N: oude slave *kloeke jongen*, C 2636 67	Date of death on: on Wednesday 10.08.1785	
Jasmin	1806	Vonnis
Jeck	1814	'Lyfeigen van Isaak Rossouw Danielzoon'/ Vonnis
Jeck (As above)	1819	'Lyfeigen van Isaac Rossouw'/ Vonnis
Jeck	1847	Game seller Death notice
Jek	1798	Johan Abraham Moes transferred him to Carel Folg or Volg
Jek	1801	Christian Johan Michiel August Kiesewetter v.Bosenberg
Jephta	1791	Vonnis
Job	Around1800	
Jobique	F?/1678	
Jochem	30 1699	Rachel Sinnekas, widow of Tyrensz Nieuwenhuysen; Price & buyer not known
Johanna	20 1699	Liberated by Hillegonda Cranendonck (widow of Marten van
Johanna VS	1762	Married Willem Jan of Macassar VS/ Jan's 2 marriage with Anna Maria v. Java VS 1779
Johanna VS	1767	Married Jan of Ceylon VS
Johanna	1771	Testament
Johanna	1771	Will; Wife of Jan Willem van Macassar
Johanna	1779	
Johanna	1785	Married Adam Harber/daughter =Christina (1765)
Johanna Maria VS	1760	Married Johan Diedrik Kinneke
Johanna (As above) MariaVS	1775	Widow of Johannes Kinneke married Jacob Heinrich Wagenaar (Rostock)

Johanna Maria	1774	Testament	
Johanna Maria	1774	Will; JM=wife of Johan Diedrich Konnecke	
Johanna Maria	1777	Married Friedrich Baumgaarden (Boomgaard)	
Johanna Maria	1778	Will; JM=wife of Fredrik Boomgaarden	
Johannes Jans		Wife, Rosetta v. Bengale vdk?/ their son, Johannes Jans Jacobus (burger) married Helena Duuring vdk daughter of Daniel Duuring	
Johannes VS	1742	Married Antonetta v. Madagascar VS	
Johannes	1763	Testament	
Johannes	1763	Will+of wife, Antonetta v. Macassar	
Johannes	1774	Testament of his widow, Anthonetta v de Westcust	
	1777	Will of Avd West Cust	
Johannes	1777	Testament of his widow, Anthonetta v de Westcust	
Johannes	1777	Will	
Johannes Jansen	1758 1770	Married Dorothea vBoegiesVS +Dorothea vCeylonVS	
Johannes Jansen		Daughter of JJ +wife Dorothea vCeylon, Ida Theodora Jansen married Dietrich Andreas Kehler in 1793	
Johannes Willems	1765	Her daughter, Deborah (Willems) vdk, married Franz Brende	
Johannes, Willem(se) VS	1756	Married Jacoba v Ceylon	
Jordaan	1739	Vonnis	
Joseph	20 1695	Cornelis Keeleman	Jan Direcx de Beer
Joseph	- 1699	Adriaan v.d.Stel	To his brother, Jonker Frans v.d. Stel
Joseph	1732	Vonnis	
Joost	1/1678		manumitted
Josias	1675		
Jouman	1825	'Te Dinapore in Bengalen geboren' /Vonnis	
Jourdaan	1738	Led a group of slaves to escape	
Juliana	1799	Freed by Jean Martin, Executor of estate of Gabriel Exter	

Juriana Frederika	1789	Extramarrital with ex-master Adam /Kind=Eva Catharina
Julenda	Registered 1824 When 61	
Julij vBeng	1749 'competent age' (*zijnde van competenten ouderdom*)	Bondsman of farmer Jan Lategaan/ thrashed a slavin on order of master; master freed & Julij was sold to another master
Julij	1794	Vonnis
July	1799	Gerhardus Nicolaas Jacobse transferred her to Johannes Michgo
July	1801	David Kuuhl
Kallae, *skool*, male, too young, unknown, N : *skool jongen*, C 2596 64	death on: on Tuesday 22.03.1774	
Karrimmedie, male, slave healthy, seasoned, *kloeke jongen*, C 2602 5	Date of death on: on Monday 21.08.1775	
Kermis	1718	Vonnis
Klass/ M	1723	
Klaas Gerrits	160s-1680s?	Married Sara van Zaloor/Solor in 1686/ daughter, Henrietta, married Muller
Keloeloe male, slave healthy, newly arrived, unknown, N: *kloeke jongen nieuwe slaven*, C 2638 27	death on: on Wednesday 31.05.1786	

Johan Christiaan Wrensch

Kombollo male, slave healthy, newly arrived, unknown, N: *kloeke jongen nieuwe slaven*, C 2638 27	Date of death on: on Tuesday 30.05.1786		
Komaboe, male, slave healthy, newly arrived, N : *kloeke jongen nieuwe slaven*, C 2638 27	death on: on Wednesday 31.05.1786		
Kupido	16 1695	Jan Suijdwijck	Simon v.d. Stael
La Fleur	1796	Vonnis	
Lafleur	1800	Johan Georg Matthias Gmehle transferred slave to Johan Martin Kelber	
Lakey	1806	Application to free slave, Philida of Bengal	
Lakey	1806	Application to free slave, Tona of Bengal	
Laky	1819	Manumission of a female slave	
Laquey	1798	Carel Gustaph von Bratt transferred him to Georg W. Hoppe	
Leentje + 2 children	1795	Retired Stellenbosch Landdrost Hendrik L. Bletterman transferred them to Clerk of Orphan Chamber Godfried Andries Watermeyer	
Lena	1728		Freed by Cecilia of Macassar
Lendor	1798	Johan Ernst v. Olnhausen transferred slave to Jacob Hendriksen	
Lendor	1799	Jacob Hendrikse transferred him to David Johan Huisman	
Lender (free black)	1816	Orphan Chamber's Request	re: Lender's estate
Lendor	1817	Liquidation & Distribution Account	
Lendor	1832	Liquidation & Distribution Account	
Lijsbeth	1680s?	Also known as Lijsbeth v. die Kaap	

Lijsje	10 1693		
Lijsje	10/11 1693	Captain Jan de Wit	C.J.Simons
	11/12 1694	Cornelis Simons	Mattthijs Wichmans
Lindor vBeng/ Same as L.vMallebaar?	1793	Had sex wiith daughter of owner, Pieter Domus/ Life sentence on Robben	
Lindor	1816	Liquidation & Distribution Account	
Lourens	1692	Same as Louis van Bengale?	
Louis	1681	Free black	
Louis	1697	Testament	
Louis	1694	Married Rebecca v. Macassar	
Louis (free settler)	1702	Included in a List +with wife, Rebecca v. Macassar +2 children in Cape District	
Louisa, Willemina	1795	Wife of Hendrik Nieman Will	
Lubin	1801	Dirk Johannes v.Dyk	Carel Christiaan Schmidt
Lubyn	1818	'Lyfeigen van John Osmond'/Vonnis	
Lucas	1767	Married Johanna Elizabeth v. Boegies VS ex-slave of Hermanus v Wieling/ k=Abraham Lucas.	
Lucas	1781	Testament	
Lucas	1781	Will +will of wife, Hanna v.Bougies	
Lucas	1783	Vonnis	
Lucas	1786	Liquidation & Distribution Account	
Lucas	1786	Liquidation & Distribution Account	
Lucia/F	24/1675		
Lucretia	1712?	Married Jan Harmen Woltering	
Luddi	9/10 Female? 1694	William Macdowall	Pierre Simond
Maart	1775	Involved in bloody fight with master, Gerrit Smit	

Maart, male, healthy, seasoned, unknown, k*loeke jongen*, C 2589 84	death on: on Tuesday 06.10.1772	
Maart	1776	Auction after death of master Johan David Kristens
Maart	1796	Suzette Nicolled transferred him to R.v.d.Riet
Maart	1807	His master applied to exchange him for 2 slaves on board Portuguese ship Restaurador
Magdilana	1687	
Magdalena	1687	Married Jan of Ternate
Magdalena		De facto marriage with Fortuin v. Boegies/ k= Maria Magdalena 1742
Magdalena	1695?	Married? Pieter Coechien VS
Magdalena v. Bengale VS	1762	Married Andries v Bengale VS
Magdalena	1770	Testament
Magteld Maria Cornelisse v. Bengale	1691	Was married to Gerrit Willemse (white) (Keeuwaarden)
Malati, Malatie	1800	Jan Michiel Stohrer as empowered by Jacobus Bierman transferred her to Dina Margaretha v. Dyk
Malati	1811	Vonnis
Mamollada *skool,*: male, newly arrived, too young, unknown, N: *skool jongen nieuwe slaven*, C 2638 27	Date of death on: on Wednesday 31.05.1786	
Manissa	1826	Will (M=wife of Ontong of Batavia
Manika vBeng	1749/ age 60	Wife of Reijnier vMadgas/ bondsman of heirs of Matthijs Krugel
Manniko	22 1700	Jacob Lucas Isaq Schriver from Batavia
Margareta/F	2months 1680	

Manuel	elderly			Promised freedom & denied it
Mercuriius	12/13 1691	Albert Fransz	William Padt	
Marcus	20 1683			
Maria	23/24 1691	Hans Hendrik Smit	Julius Lasius	
Maria	1658			
Maria	1687	ExtraMar with Hans Rutger Troost (Duitsland) /Maria was freed by Troost 1687/ k=Carel Henrdik		
Maria	1691	Married Domingo van Bengale		
Maria	27/28 1696	Jan Coenraad Visscher	Freed with 3 children	
Maria /F	18 1697	Jean Buys	Jan Brommert	
Maria	1702	Mentioned in a List of Cape District + husband, Domingo v. Bengal		
Maria	1710	widow of Isaak VS, Married Frans Verkouter		
Maria	1712	Wife of Domingo of Bengal 1712	Wil 1	
Maria	1739	Daughter, Anna Willemse, married Joachim Ernst Wepener 1739		
Maria		Grand daughter, Anna Susanna Wepener, married Jan Willem Wilkens/ Jan's 2 marriage		
Maria		Daughter, Susana Visser, married Hans Hendrik Hatting in 1716		
Maria	23 186	Jan Brommert	Reynier Evertse	
Maria VS	1793	Married Pieter Langeraads of Amsterdam		
Maria	1798	Gave power of attorney to	William Kolver	
Maria	1798	Legacy recd from late Gerrit Jan van den Kerkhoff		
Maria	1811	Fortuyn of Ceylon appl. To emancipate slave		
Maria	1822	Will (wife of Baksoe v. Bengalen		
Maria	1829	Wife of Jeck v.d.Kaap/Will		
Maria		ExtraMar with Willem Teerling		

Maria Johanna	1777	Testament	
Maria Johanna	1777	Will; MJ=wife of Jacob Wagener	
Maria Oelofs (widow of Adrian Smuts)	1806	Applied to free slave, Philander of Bengal	
Martha	14 1698	William Erle	Maria Everts
Matthijs	21/22 1691	Jan Barentsz	Sara de Roo
Matthijs	12/13 1695	Hermanus Almina	Christoffel Hasewinckel
Matthijs	27 1700	Jacob Lundsen	Hercules v. Loon
Meij	1775	Vonnis	
Mentor	1799	Carel Valentyn Folg transferred him to Sybrand Dormehl	
Mercurius	12 1691		
Mercurius	12/13 1692	Willem Padt	Barent Borchard
Mercuur	1791	Vonnis	
Metsilla: male, healthy, newly arrived, unknown, N: *kloeke jongen nieuwe slaven*, C 2638 27	death on: on Thursday 11.05.1786		
Mey	1799	Roelof Roelofsen transferred her to John M. Kelber	
Mietje	1820	Will	
Mina	1798	'Free man' Amon of Macasser transferred her to Pieter Francois Theron	
Montfort	15/16 1690	Albert Fokkes	Jacob Joppe
Mosis	1712	Vonnis	

Nawakorare Lodge: *skool*, female, newly arrived, too young, unknown, N : *skool meijd, nieuwe slaven,* C 2638 27	Date of death on: on Saturday 27.05.1786		
Neptunus November v Beng	1753	Vonnis	
November	1798	Jean Charles De la Harre +1	Jacob Singuir
October	1807	Vonnis	
Onverwagt	1797	Carel Rebender transferred slave to Willem v. Doesburg	
Orange	22/23	Jacob Joppe de Jonge	Jansz de Wereld
Orsson	22' 1697	Jan Direx d. Beer	Marten Pousion
Pacolet	22 1697	Christoffel Groenewalt	Jan Lamberts Meijburgh
Panay (free black)	1810	Applied to free slave boy Antony	
Paris	24/1674		
Paris	1726	Vonnis	
Pasquael	1669		
Pasquaal	1/1678		
Pasquael	1679		
Patientie	1804	Vonnis	
Pedro from Dhaca Bengal	14 1698	Hendrik Donker	Jan v. Meerland
Pedro	1756	Vonnis	
Pedro	1764		
Pedro	1798	Andries J. Beck transferred him to Andreas Gotz	
	1800	Petrus Echardt empowered by Andreas Gotz transferred him to Michael Hogan	

Pesar	13/7/1745 Death Bandiet en Jongen		
Petro	12 1695	Thomas Evans for Joan de Klerck	Jan Feuber
Petronella	18 1699	Liberated by Hillegonda Cranendonck	
Petrus VS	1765	Married Flora v. Rio de la Goa VS	
Philander	1791	Vonnis	
Philander	1799	Carel Hendrik Martheze transferred him to Alexander Farquhar	
Philander	1800	Johan Christiaan Schultz transferred him to Jan Frederik Hartong	
Philander	1806	See Maria Oelofs	
Philander	1816	Will + Also will of wife, Sophia v. Pontecherie (2CNA257/267)	
Philander	1835	His widow's Liquidation & Distribution Account (widow=Sophia of Pontecherie)	
Philander	1835	Inventory + Inventory of wife=Sophia (2CNA259/267)	
Philander	1835	List of property +List of property of wife= Sophia of Pondichery	
Philemon	1797	Anthony Krynauw to Stephanus Jacobus Botha	
Philidor	1801	Vonnis	
Piet	1810	His master, Maria Carolina Ryghard applied to free him	
Pieter	13/14 1670		
Pieter			
Pieter	1686		
Pieter	20 1690	Jacob Cool	Jan Direx De Beer
Pieter	20/21 1692	Jan Hanegrif	Guilliam Heems
Pieter VS	1725	Married 1 Delphina vdKus VS 1725 + 2Johanna Sara Sol 1747+ 3 Helena vd Kus VS 1756	
Pieter	1726	Testament	
Pieter	1745	Testament	
Pieter	1745	Will + will of Delphina vd Cust=wife	

Pieter	1746	Testament
Pieter	1747	Testament
Pieter	1747	Will
Peter	1756	Testament
Pieter	1759	Will + will of wife, Helena vd Cust
Pieter	1768	Testament
Pieter	1775	Will
Pieter		Daughter Maria Elizabeth Pieterse vdk married Frans Hendrik Stapelberg in 1776
Pieter	1799	Jonathan Brown transferred slave to Albrecht Dell
Pieter	1829	Insolvent Liquidation & Distribution Account
Pieter	1830	Record of proceedings of 'illiquid' case re: debt
Pieter Pieterse	1774	Married? Helena vd Kus/ 'Liebbrandt Req 2'
Piet Snap	20 1683	Hendrik Janse bonte Kraai
Philida	1796	Notarial protocol: Philida's declaration about Christoffel Linker involving wife of Linker & slave, Kaatje, who has a bastard child
Philida	1800	Johannes Heyne transferred him to Johan Michael Bertholt
Philida Pieter v. Bengale	1806	Her master, Lakey, applied to free her
Plato	1809	Vonnis
Present	1799	Jacob Hendrikse transferred her to S. Roelo Helsing
Rachel	1736	Wife of Christian Thomas van die Kus, baptized their 5 children during a period of 9 years
Rachel VS	1737 +1741	Married Christian Thomas vd Kus VS
Rama	1806	Her master, Gerrit Deneijss applied to free her
Ramma Rampie	1797	Jam Bolleurs transferred her to Jan Abraham Hell
Regina	1779 baptized in Tulbagh	When Reg. was baptized as adult/ex-slave of Arnoldus Vosloo/ was de facto wife of Matthys Albregtse Children= Willem & Matthys
Rammij	1791	Vonnis
Rammijenni, male, *kloeke jongen*, C 2588 118	death on: Saturday 18.07.1772	

Rebecca	1744	(MOOC8/6.74, 1744). See Carel Jansz among slave owners
Rebecca		Daughter Appolonia Jansz vdk married Frederik Simon Plaagman 1751 1751
Rebecca	1776	With 5 children (Maij, Saje, Sarie, Sogie, & Salie (all from Cape) auctioned after Death of master Johan David Kristens (Ref. MOOC8/16.28)
Regina		Daughter Margaretha du Plooy married Wolf Friedrich von Ruhberg (Duitsland)
Regina	1781	Liquidation & Distribution Account
Regina	1787	Vonnis
Regina	No date	Ex-slave, married to master, Hendrik Wilkem du Plooy
Maria Elizabeth du Plooy		Daughter of Regina vBengale extramarital to Abel Erasmus
Robert Robi/ Ruby	1808	His master, Coenraad Johannes Gie, applied to free him
Roebie	1801	Freed by Jan Daniel Alders & Anthonie Nix, Executors of estate of late Hermanus Coen
Roebie (freed slave)	1802	Bond of security given by Dietloff Ree & Christoffel Rantel
Rosalina		Daughter Johanna Christina vd Sayn married Johan Joorst Steenberg
Rosa		
Rosa VS	1749	Married Abraham (Kaap)
Rosalyn VS	1737	Married Johannes Jansen (Ceylon)/baptized 5 children
Roselyn	1731-1740	Baptized her 5 children between 1731-40. Her master, vryswart Jacobus Hendriksz v.d. Kus, fathered children.
Roseleyn	1758	Testament
Roselijn	1758	Will
Rosetta		ExtraMarital with Johannes of Ceylon/ k=Johannes
Rosetta	1750	Will; R=wife of Johannes Jansz
Rosetta	1750	Will;R=wife of JJ
Rosetta	1764	Will;R=wife of JJ
Rosetta	1757	Will; R=wife of Arend van Balij
Rosetta	1758	Widow of Arend Balie, married Johannes Hansen of Batavia

Rosetta		HusbandJan Janse of Ceylon/ their daughter Maria Sultania or Maria Juliana Jansen vdk married Jan Hendrik Christoffel Schmidt 1760
Rosetta	1767	Swapped for Anthony
Rosetta	1767?	Married? Jonas of Batavia
Rosetta	1769	Widow of Jan Jansz of Ceylon / Liquidation & Distribution A/C
Rosetta	1784	Testament
Rosetta	1784	Will/Wife of Harman Aarts
Rosetta	1784	Will; R=wife of Harman Aarts
Rosetta	1840	servant Death notice
Rosette	1764	Testament
Roset	1840	Death notice
Rosina		Extramrital Rel with Valentyn of Macassar/ k= Cornelia Valentyn 1773
Rosina Cornelia	1782	Marriage (?) with Jan Dirkse/ daughter Carolina
Rozet/F	1809	Her master, Pieter Andriessen, applied to free her
Sabina+1	1802	Notarial protocol—Obligation re: Sybrand Abraham de Beer to Jacobus Louw about posting the 2 slaves as security
Salatria or Salatria	1796	Suzette Nicolled transferred her to R. v.d.Riet
Salinda	1799	Carel Godfried Landwerth transferred her to Johan Hendrik Wolff
Samieta + child Regina of Cape	1801	Surgeon Christiaan August Bosenberg transferred her to Jacob Naude
Samita	1819	
Samuel, Christoffel VS	1790	Married Maria vdk
Sara	20 1699	Lambert Jan Lispensier Simonsz
Sara	1713-1719	Baptised 4 children/ Master=Willem ten Damme/ Father of children Floris Jacobs(?)
Schot Robert	1720	Will + wife Cicilia of Madagascar's will
Schot, Robert	1741	Liquidation & Distribution Account
Scipio alias Kees		

Scipio	1726	Vonnis	
Scipio Africanus	1668	Hired as slave by Angela v. Bengale	
Sebastiana VS	1718	Married Abraham VS (Maccasar)	
Selvea	1839	Death notice	
September		Married? Magdalena v. Batavia/ k= Magdalena 1708 freed? Baptism witnesses= Otto Ernst v Graan + Rachel vdKus	
September	1708	Baptized his child, Magdalene	
September	1802	Notarial protocol re:Obligation involving Johannes to Nicolaas Seeberg about purchase of September	
Servidor	12 1692	William Price	Roelof Diodati
Silvia	1798	Johannes Eberhardt transferred her to Frederik Preller	
Silvia	1814	SW Echardt requested to emancipate her	
Silvie	1798	Catharina Adriana Brand transferred her to Gideon Malherbe	
Simon	19/20 1691	Matthijs Michielsz	Direk de Beer
Simon/M	24 1696		
Simon As above?	1696	Joris v.Straaten	Jan Cotze
Simon Death Sunday 04.12.1740 Sijmon, assumed in Lodge, male, slave healthy, seasoned, unknown, N: C 2490 52	24/25 *kloeke jongen,*	Jan Cotze	Hendrik Mulder
Simon	1801	Carel Folg	Jacob v.d. Waereld
Simon Hansze	1700?	60 years freed?	
Smaudi	1820	Will +will of wife, Candaca of Bougies	
Sol, Johan-na Sara	1747	Will of Wife of Pieter van Bengalen; Sol's identity not mentioned	
Solon	1767	Vonnis	

Sophia de Lodriga VS	1725	Alias Flo . . . ?/ married Carel Jansen of Ceylon VS	
Sophia As below?	1798	Estard A. Grimbeeck	Georg Frederik Goetz
Sophie+2 children, Louis & Rebecca, both of Cape	1799	George Frederik Goetz transferred S+2 to Johannes Vos	
Susanna	1673?		
Susanna/F	1680		
Susanna/F	20 1697		
As above	20 1697	Simon v.d. Stel for Willem ten Rhijne in Batavia	Hendrick Munckerus
	20 1796	Hendrick Munckerus	Susanna Lubberinck
Susanna van Een Oor v Beng.	Executed		
Tano, Jan Vogelvanger VS	1759	Married Clara van Batavia	
Tano, Jan	1766	Testament	
Tano, Jan	1777	Testament	
Telemachus	1794	Vonnis	
Thomas Baile	1796	John Stuart gave power of attorney to Baile	
Thomas	25/1671	RDrs70?	
Thomas	20/1671		
Thomas			
Thomas	22/1672		
Thomas	1678		
Thomas /M	18 1698		
	18 1698	Cornelis Overraat	Hans Hendrik Smit
	18 1698	Hans Hendrik Smit	HendrikJansz v.Kempen

Thomas	1714	Vonnis		
Titus/M	1680	Partner of Catrina		
Titus	1714	Maria Mouton		Executed
Titus	1722	Michael Otto or Ox		
Titus	23 1687			
Titus	12 1690	Boudewijn Claesz	Nicolaas Laupser	
Titus	19/20 1693	Harmen Voet	Jan Cotze	
Titus	20 1695	Jacob Landsheer	Simon v.d. Stael	
Titus	25 1695	Elsje v. Suurwaerden	Arijen v. *Wijck*	
Titus	27 1697	Pieter v.Eeden	Henning Husing	
Titus	14 1697	Hendrick van Burtenhem	Henning	
Titus	18/19 1700	Rutgert Mensinck	Jan . . . (potter living near Salt River)	
Titus	24 1700	Simon Witboom	Jacobus de Wet	
Titus	27/28 1700	Octavius from Macassar	Jacob (free black from Coromandel)	
Titus	18.11.1727 Death notice	*Volwasse slaf*		
Titus	1761	Vonnis		
Tob ('the freed slave)	1798	Bond of security given by Cornelis Cruywagen		
Toemasse	20/1676			
Tona	1806	Her master, Lakey, applied to free her		
Willemsen, Johannes (slave?)	1764	Testament		
Valentijn	1742	Vonnis		
Ventura/F	1678	manumitted		

Venus	1749	Maria Pietersz	Gifted to Jan Rogier van Morslen
Willem	1666		
Wilhelmina	1793		Married ex-master Hendrik Niemand (Duitsland)/ K=
Louisa VS			Maria Geertruida =12/12/97 (adult) died?
Zeebouwer	1815		Petition re:his freedom

Nnis

Total= ± 691
Politics of the Past ed. Bu Gathercole & Lowenthal

Appendix D

Inventory of Bengali Slave Owners in the Cape
(in alphabetical order)

Achilles (free black)	1799	Christoffel Coenraad transferred slave Soenting to him		CNA126/206	
Achilles(free black)	1816	Requested permission to manumit a female slave		2CNA011/267	memorial
Achilles (a tallowchandlier)	1833	Listed in Bank's inventory of free black slave owners in Cape Town		Bank, Slavery, Inventory, p.236	Had 6 slaves
Achillis	1816	Request to free his slave		CNA38/206	
Angela ('widow of Arnoldus Willems')	1698	Pieter v.Malabar (22) sold to Angela by William Erle		Boeseken, Slaves & Free.P185	Rds50
Andries V S	1762	Married Magdalena v Beng VS			
Anna de Koningh					
Anthoni 'vrij ingesetene alhier' (free local resident)	1676	Baddou From Bali	Governor Bax Rds.50	Boeseken132	Rds.50
As above	1678	Paul sold to Anthonij ('free burgher')	Aletta Hinlopen Rds.100	Boeseken	
Anthonij Free burgher	1683	Slave Pouwlus sold to Oeloff Bergh by Orphan Masters from estate of dead Anthonij		Boeseken140	
Antony VS	1751	Married Wilhelmina v. Maccasar		Heese Groep 81	
Anthony Jansz	1676	Maria from Malabar	Slooper Rds.35	Boeseken132	Rds.35
Betje	1817	Application to free a female slave		2CNA12/267	
Betje (a free Woman)	1817	Application to free a slave		2CNA14/267	

Betje	1833	Listed in Bank's inventory of free black slave owners in Cape Town	Bank, slavery, List, p.237	Had 1 slave
Bietja (freed slave woman)	1800	Contract bet her & Frederik Lilie re: Slave Apeil Simauba	CNA83/206	
P. Brueys (ex-slave?)	1795		CNA58/206	
Caatje (Free woman)	1798	Slave Laquay transferred to her by free black Marthins Jacobus	CNA113/206	
Canterbury/ Canterbory/ Canterborry (free black)	1800	Obligation to Egidius Benedictus Ziervogel	CNA66/206	Posted as security
Carel Jansz van Bengalen	1744	requested in his will that his slave, Rebecca of Bengalen and her two children, Jan and Appollonia of the Cape, be freed at his death. It was also stated in the inventory that Rebecca and her children inherited the young slave, Anthony of Coutchin	(MOOC8/6.74, 1744).	
Catharina	1713	Wife of Jan Willemsen Will	2CNA98/267	
Catharina VS	1735	Married Frans Hendrik Mark (Duitsland)		
Catharina ('vry swartin')	1790	Testament	2CNA49/267	
Catharina Opkhim VS	1702			
Christina VS	1735	Married Frans Hendrik Mark (Duitsland)	Heese Groep 587	
Claas Gerritsz	1686	Pieter from Madag. (20/22) sold by Will Deeron to Cl. Gerritsz	Boeseken, Slaves & Free Blacks, p.145	Rds.55
Cornelis('N vryswarte')	1731	Testament	2CNA70/267	
Cupido	1833	Listed in Bank's inventory of free black slave owners in Cape Town	Bank, Slavery, Inventory p.237	Had 1 slave
Damon (free black)	1796	Transferred slave Diana to free black Letjon of Baly	CNA95/206	

Daniel	1833	Listed in Bank's inventory of free black slave owners in Cape Town	Bank, Slavery, Inventory, p.237	Had 1 slave
David (free black)	1800	Adam Jacobs empowered by Pieter Pieterse transferred slave Achilles of Macassar to David	CNA145/206	
David	1810	Appl. to emancipate Slave April van Mallabaar	2CNA007/267	memorial
David (free black)	1817	Requesting permission to free a slave	2CNA15/267	
David (free black slave owner	1833	Listed in Bank's inventory of free black slave owners in Cape Town	Bank, Slavery, Inventory, p.236	Had 10 slaves
Domingo	1692	Free black	Borrowed f300 from Church funds at 6%. Repaid 25.8.1694	
Domingo ('den Chinees Domingo)	1698	Cupido (16) from Naga-patnam to Domingo	By Hans Hendrik Smit Rds70	Boeseken185
Domingo 'Chinaman'	1698	Pieter (16) from Malabar sold to Domin	By HansHendrik Smit Rds70	Boeseken, Slaves & Free, p.185
Dorothea (widow of Thoimas Pieterse(n)	1798	Transferred Cupido of Mallabar to Zacharias	CNA117/206 CNA140/206	
	1800	Herman Transferred slave Diana of Cape To Frederik Potgieter		
February	1833	Listed in Bank's inventory of free black slave owners in Cape Town	Bank, Slavery, Inventory, p.236	Had 4 slaves
Frans (free black)	1799	Christiaan Paulsen transferred slave August of Ceylon to Frans	CNA131/206	
Hanna	1798	Freed slave, Zaida of Cape	CNA74/206	
	1798	Freed slave, Camies of Cape	CNA75/206	

Hector	1833	Listed in Bank's inventory of free black slave owners in Cape Town	Bank, Slavery, Inventory, p.237	Had 2 slaves
Isaac VS	1702	Name in List+wife, Maria v.Coromandel	eGGSA p.12	
Isaacs Albert VS	1761	Married ex-mistress Helena v.Ceylon	Heese Groep79-81	
Jack (a retailer)	1833	Listed in Bank's inventory of free black slave owners in Cape Town	Bank, Slavery, Inventory, p.236	Had 4 slaves
Jansen Hendrik VS	1773	Married Sylvia Maria v. Madagascar	Heese Groep79	
January(free black)	1817	Application for permission to free a slave	2CNA13/267	
January	1833	Listed in Bank's inventory of free black slave owners in Cape Town	Bank, Slavery Inventory, p.236	Had 4 slaves
January (free black?)	1857	Death notice	2CNA27/267	
Johan Adriaans	1833	Listed in Bank's inventory of free black slave owners in Cape Town	Bank, Slavery, Inventory p.237	Had 2 slaves
July	1833	Listed in Bank's inventory of free black slave owners in Cape Town	Bank, Slavery, Inventory, p.237	Had 1 slave
Lakey	1799	Marthinus Jacobus transferred slave Moses of Cape	CNA121/206	
Lakey	1833	Listed in Bank's inventory of free black slave owners in Cape Town	Bank, Slavery, Inventory, p.236	Had 4 slaves
Lindor	1833	Listed in Bank's inventory of free black slave owners in Cape Town	Bank, Slavery, Inventory, p.237	Had 1 slave
Louis	1687	Matthijs from Java (27/28) sold by Adriaan v. Brakel to Louis	Boeseken, Slavery & Free Blacks, p.150	Rds35

Louis 'swarte landbouwer'	1689	Matthijs From Malabar (33/34) sold by Louis	Abraham De Hartogh	Boeseken154 + Boes, Slaves &, p113	Rds.30
Louis	1697	Titus from Samoa 22 sold to Louis by	Philibert v. Boesschot	Boeseken178	Rds53
Maria	1801	Notarial protocol re: will of Pieter Langeraats &Maria		2CNA20/267	
Pannaay	1833	Listed in Bank's inventory of free black slave owners in Cape Town		Bank, Slavery, Inventory, p.237	Had 1 slave
Pieter VS		His ex-slave, Francina Jansz vdk married to Andries Meyer of Danzig (Cf Elizabeth Rebecca		Heese, Groep59	
Pieter v. Bengale	1710	Was a slave of Governor WA V. der Stel; later a vryswarte; then hired as a knecht by Angela vBeng		Kinders185	
Pieter(slave?)	1832	Record of proceedings of provisional case: Pieter vs.Jacob v. Reenen		2CNA26/267	
Rachel	1737 & 1741				
Rebecca					
Rosina	1833	Listed in Bank's inventory of free black slave owners in Cape Town		Bank, Slavery, Inventory, p237	Had 2 slaves
Schot, Robert	1724	Kontrak/ 'Vryswarte'		2CNA252/267	
Willemina Louisa	1795	Notarial protocol re: will of Hendrik Nieman & Willemina		2CNA19/267	

Total Bengali slave owners = 59

Appendix E

Genealogical Chart Showing Therese Benadé's Descent from Angela van Bengale

Angela van Bengale = *Unknown husband (or partner)*
⬇
Anna de Koning = Olof Bergh
⬇
Marthinus
⬇
Olof Marthinus
⬇
Olof
⬇
Olof Marthinus
⬇
Olof Marthinus
⬇
Olof Marthinus
⬇
Olof Marthinus
⬇
Olof Marthinus
⬇
Anna Helena Frederika Bergh
⬇
Petronella van Zijl
⬇
Therese Benadé
(*Informant of the present author*)

Therese Benadé is the author of Anna, Dogter van Angela van Bengale, *which was published by David Philip of South Africa in 2004. An English translation,* Kites of Good Fortune, *David Philip, came out in 2005. Therese Benadé may be contacted at* <http://www.theresebenade.com/index.htm>

Appendix F

Portrait of Anna de Koning Displayed at Groot Constantia

Appendix G

Bengali Slaves being Sold at Pipli in the Hoogli District.

<http://www.atlasofmutualheritage.nl/detail.aspx?page=dafb&lang=en&id=2022>

Appendix H

A Sketch of Hoogli

< http://www.atlasofmutualheritage.nl/detail.aspx?page=dafb&lang=en&id=3462>

Appendix I

A Letter Written by a Slave in Buginese.

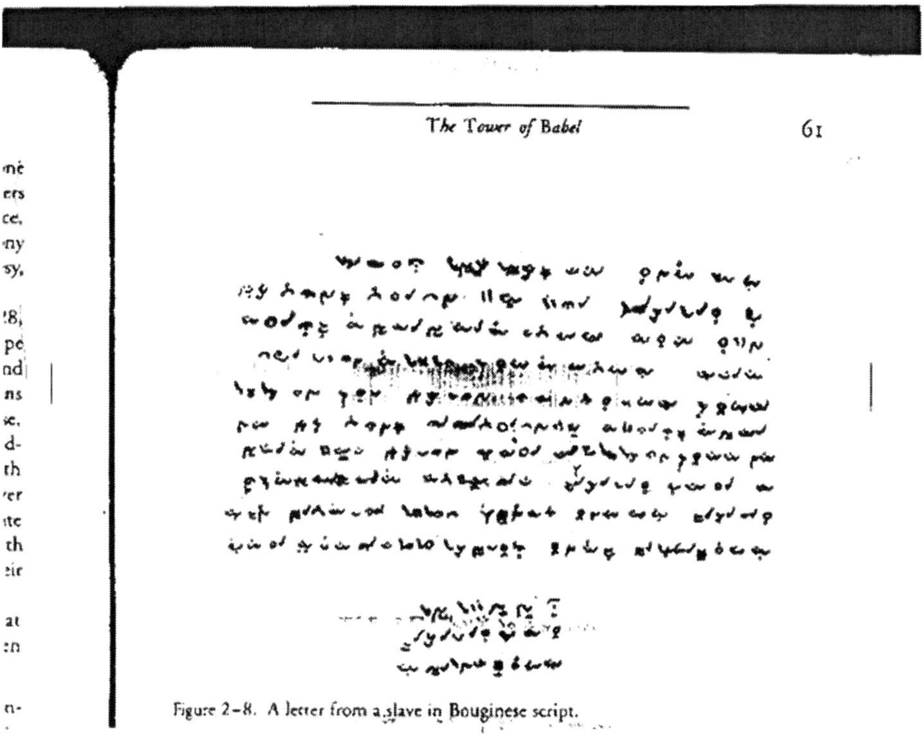

The Tower of Babel   61

Figure 2-8. A letter from a slave in Bouginese script.

Robert Shell, *Children of Bondage*, p. 61

Index

W

Lightning Source UK Ltd.
Milton Keynes UK
UKOW02f1815230616

276939UK00001B/93/P